Astrology for Winners

ASTROLOGY
FOR
WINNERS

Horse Races and Racing Planets

John Savarese

Published by John Savarese
July 2016, New York City
Author: John Savarese
ISBN: 978-0-692-75487-0
Website: www.astrologyforwinners.com

The Solar Fire Fagan-Allen sidereal astrology system and Campanus house astrological charts in this book were created using Solar Fire v9.0 astrology software (www.alabe.com).

The Janus Western Sidereal (Fagan-Bradley) sidereal astrology system and Campanus house astrological speculums and charts in this book were created using Janus astrology software v4.3 (www.astrology-house.com).

Front Cover Photo: Anne M. Eberhardt. Midday sprinting towards the finish line with Pure Clan in hot pursuit.

Contents

Preface

This book provides the tools you need to pick a horse with the tendency to be the winner in a thoroughbred or harness race as these races have numbered post positions in their starting gates (in this book, we focus on thoroughbred racing). Basically you will need to create a chart of the race using the date, place and time of the race before the actual day of the race. You must then analyze this chart using the guidelines set forth in this book, including the use of lunar mansions, in order to see the planetary body in the most powerful position in the chart. This planetary body has a post position number in the race. You then pick the horse in that post position, and you support picking this horse using the information in this book.

I would like to thank Count Gramalkin, foremost proponent and principal advocate of the San Francisco School of Sidereal Astrology of John Mazurek for his insights into putting astrology to work as a gambling tool. Count Gramalkin is the prime heir of Cyril Fagan, the founder of Sidereal Astrology, and of John Mazurek, Cyril Fagan's best student and most esteemed colleague. John Mazurek formulated the astrological technique of picking horse race winners using planetary bodies and post positions, and he wrote several other significant astrological works as well. Count Gramalkin actually witnessed John Mazurek pick five winners in a row at the track using the technique. With diligence and persistence, some knowledge of handicapping races (references to learn and/or to get this information are provided herein), and a bit of luck (chapter 7), you will have an excellent chance of picking horses that have the tendency to win.

—*John Savarese, B.A. Syracuse University 1972, M.A. City University of New York, Hunter College 1974, NCGR-PAA (National Council for Geocosmic Research-Professional Astrologers' Alliance) Level 3*

July 2016, New York City

This book is dedicated to John Mazurek, 1919-2003, who embodied every quality of what it means to be a great astrologer.

Disclaimer

Please note that the information provided in this book is not intended to encourage gambling and is for informational purposes only. In this book, I am speaking of tendencies for a horse to win, not certainties for a horse to win so realize there is always a chance to not win. Gamble at your own risk. I make no claims as to success from using the information in this book. I am not able to offer guarantees as to the outcomes from using this book and I absolve myself and my business entities from any possible losses incurred by anyone as a result of following the instructions contained in this book. Also, if gambling is a problem or addiction, please consult an appropriate medical professional.

Chapter 1

THE WIN STRATEGY

The basic principle of the WIN strategy is that planetary bodies in our solar system are assigned post position numbers. The astrologer John Mazurek from his experience of betting on winning horses assigned post position numbers to these planetary bodies. Each number assigned to a planetary body is a post position in the starting gate of a race. You create an astrological chart named the "Post Time Event Chart" by John Mazurek of the race on which you want to wager, using the date, place and post time of the race. You then analyze this chart to see its most powerful planetary body, and note the post position assigned to this planetary body. The horse in that post position will have an excellent tendency to win the race. Supported with the additional information supplied in this book, you will be confident in placing bets on the horse.

Chapter 2

PLANETARY BODIES AND THEIR ASSIGNED POST POSITION NUMBERS

Here are the planetary bodies and their assigned post position numbers for day races and night races:

- The Sun is 1 (4 for a night race)
- The Moon is 2 (7 for a night race)
- Mercury is 5
- Venus is 6
- Mars is 9
- Jupiter is 3
- Saturn is 8
- Uranus is 4 (1 for a night race)
- Neptune is 7 (2 for a night race)

If for example Jupiter is the most powerful planet in the chart of a day race, you would pick the horse in the third post position to have an excellent chance of winning the race. There can be fourteen or so races in a racing day card. As you can see, you can only bet races that have a field of nine or fewer horses (not like the Kentucky Derby which might have a field of 15 or more horses). Post positions in a race are given to horses by random draw, and post positions start at post position one at the rail. Each assigned post position given to a horse becomes the track program number of the horse in any online or hardcopy program guide list of the horses in the race, for instance if a horse was given post position one in the draw, the track program number of the horse is 1 so the horse becomes the 1 horse at the top of the program. The track program number of a horse is also shown on the saddle cloth of the horse under the saddle. For track program number 1 in any race, the saddle cloth is always red with the white number 1 on it.

In the field of a race, you might see a two-part or even three-part entry from the same owner where for example in the program of the race, there is a track program number 1 for a horse and a track program number 1A for the other horse in the two-part entry. It is important to note that the 1 horse and the 1A horse might not have the first post position and second post position, unless they received these post positions in the draw. They will retain the original post positions they got from the draw, say the fourth post position and the seventh post position. In this case, mention of these fourth and seventh post positions will be provided in the text for these horses in the program of the race.

To stay on top of two-part entries in the race you want to bet, on a separate piece of paper, write the name of the horse that is the first part of the entry from the online or hardcopy Daily Racing Form (DRF), hardcopy booklet program of the race at the track, or in the online Equibase. Then under that name, write the name of the horse that is the second part of the entry, then the third name that is the third entry, then the fourth name that is the fourth entry, and so on until the list of names is complete. Then to the left of each name write its track program number for example 1, 2, 3, 4 etc, (and for instance from our example above, you would write 1 and 1A to the left of the names of the two horses in the two-part entry). Then to the left of each track program number, write the post position number of the horse. The entries in the list of the hardcopy DRF, hardcopy booklet program or the online Equibase are listed in successive post position number order (in Equibase, the post position numbers are actually stated as such). Now for each horse in the two-part entry, write the post position number of the horse that is mentioned in the text of the horse in the program guide. Then rearrange the list in post position number order. You will then have an accurate list of post positions for all the horses in the race, including the horses in the two-part entry. This procedure is shown in the example on the next page.

The columns are post position number, track program number and the name of the horse. This list is arranged by post position number and track program number:

1	1	Jill
2	2	Harry
3	3	Carol
4	4	Ted
5	5	Pat
6	6	Ed
7	7	Jackie

There is no need to rearrange this list. There are no two-part or three-part entries and there are no scratches. It's just a normal list. No problems.

The following list that has a two-part entry which is the 1 horse and the 1A horse is arranged by track program number. The columns are post position number, track program number and the name of the horse:

4	1	Jill
7	1A	Harry
2	2	Carol
3	3	Ted
1	4	Pat
5	5	Ed
6	6	Jackie

Then rearrange the list to be in post position order:

1	4	Pat
2	2	Carol
3	3	Ted

4	1	Jill
5	5	Ed
6	6	Jackie
7	1A	Harry

Use this list for your post positions in the WIN strategy.

Horses can be scratched (taken out of a race) even right up to post time (though rare). Scratches do happen and they must be taken into account when you use the WIN strategy. If a horse is scratched in a race, the remaining horses will fill in its vacated post position in several ways. The method used by NYRA (New York Racing Association) is used at the majority of tracks. If horses are scratched in a race, the remaining horses will fill in the vacated post positions, one by one going left towards the rail. This is shown in the following NYRA example.

The list in post position number order:

1	4	Pat
2	2	Carol
3	3	Ted
4	1	Jill
5	5	Ed
6	6	Jackie (your pick)
7	1A	Harry

Ted is scratched:

1	4	Pat
2	2	Carol
~~3~~	~~3~~	~~Ted~~
4	1	Jill
5	5	Ed

6	6	Jackie (your pick)
7	1A	Harry

The new post positions:

1	4	Pat
2	2	Carol
3	1	Jill
4	5	Ed
5	6	Jackie (your pick)
6	1A	Harry

If you selected your winner Jackie in the original sixth post position from having Venus as the strongest planet in the chart of the race and the Ted horse in the third post position is scratched, the winner you picked will now be in the fifth post position. You must now change your winner to be the new horse in the sixth post position which is Harry. If you do not like Harry, you cannot bet the race.

The method used by Churchill Downs involves the remaining horses filling in the vacated post positions, one by one going right away from the rail. This is shown in the following example:

The list in post position number order:

1	4	Pat
2	2	Carol (your pick)
3	3	Ted
4	1	Jill
5	5	Ed
6	6	Jackie (your pick)
7	1A	Harry

Ted is scratched:

1	4	Pat
2	2	Carol (your pick)
~~3~~	~~3~~	~~Ted~~
4	1	Jill
5	5	Ed
6	6	Jackie
7	1A	Harry

The new post positions:

2	4	Pat
3	2	Carol (your pick)
4	1	Jill
5	5	Ed
6	6	Jackie
7	1A	Harry

If you selected your winner Carol in the original second post position from having the Moon as the strongest planet in the chart of the race and the Ted horse in the third post position is scratched, the winner you picked will now be in the third post position. You must now change your winner to be the new horse in the second post position which is Pat. If you do not like Pat, you cannot bet the race.

The method used by Golden Gate Fields, Sam Houston Park and several other tracks involves pulling the post position number of the scratched horse from the starting gate and not moving any horses:

The list in post position number order:

1	4	Pat
2	2	Carol

3	3	Ted
4	1	Jill (your pick)
5	5	Ed
6	6	Jackie
7	1A	Harry

Ted is scratched:

1	4	Pat
2	2	Carol
~~3~~	~~3~~	~~Ted~~
4	1	Jill (your pick)
5	5	Ed
6	6	Jackie
7	1A	Harry

The new post positions:

1	4	Pat
2	2	Carol
4	1	Jill (your pick)
5	5	Ed
6	6	Jackie
7	1A	Harry

Your new rearranged post positions (these are the post positions you will use in the WIN strategy), in this case:

1	4	Pat
2	2	Carol
3	1	Jill (your pick)
4	5	Ed
5	6	Jackie
6	1A	Harry

If you selected your winner Jill in the original fourth post position from having Uranus as the strongest planet in the chart of the race and the Ted horse in the third post position is scratched, the winner you picked will now be in the third post position. You must now change your winner to be the new horse in the fourth post position which is Ed. If you do not like Ed, you cannot bet the race.

The important thing to remember in the three methods is that there cannot be a gap between horses in the starting gate. You must also confirm the "filling in the post positions of scratched horses" policies at the racetracks worldwide where you want to place your bets by contacting them and jotting down their policies for future reference.

If your horse gets scratched, don't bet the race as the betting service might insert the favorite to replace your horse. To know the scratches at any time before the race, you can call HBI Bets in Toronto at 1-888-675-8886 for personalized service. For automated service, you can call 1-888-675-6337 or 1-416-623-6337. When you call automated service, you will be asked for an access code which is actually a race track code (you can type 12 followed by # to access Belmont). Then when prompted, hit # again to hear a list of racetracks and codes from which you can get the racetrack code of the racetrack you want. Then type in that code followed by # to get the scratches for the card at that racetrack. You can also get scratches on a timely basis at a board listing scratches inside a racetrack.

Chapter 3

THE MOST POWERFUL PLANETARY BODY

The planetary body that has the most points according to the guide below is the most powerful planetary body in the chart of the race. This planetary body is used to determine the post position of the horse with the greatest tendency to win. The Sun and Moon are considered planetary bodies.

- Assign two points if it is on an angle. The planetary body must be within 5 degrees of the angle, either before or after the angle. If the race post time is 12 noon, do not assign two points to the Sun as the Sun will always be on the Midheaven angle at noon. Assigning two points to the Sun in this case will give it an unfair advantage.
- If it is on an angle and it rules the sign of the angle, assign two points, or if it is exalted in the sign of the angle, assign one point.
- Assign two points if it is in the sign that it rules.
- Assign two points to a planetary body if it is in a sign that it rules and it is in the lunar mansion of this sign by degree that has Jupiter or Venus in it, for example if Mercury in the chart is within the range of degrees (zero degrees to 4 degrees 17 minutes as shown below) in the lunar mansion of Jupiter in the sign Gemini ruled by Mercury, this bodes well for Mercury in the chart and consequently the horse associated with it by post position (see the ranges of degrees for each lunar mansion in each sign below).

- Assign one point to a planetary body if it is NOT in a sign that it rules but it is in the lunar mansion of the sign by degree that has Jupiter or Venus in it, for example if Mars in the chart is within the range of degrees (4 degrees 17 minutes to 25 degrees 43 minutes as shown below) in the lunar mansion of Venus in the sign Capricorn which is not ruled by Mars, this kind of bodes well for Mars in the chart and consequently the horse associated with it by post position (see the ranges of degrees for each lunar mansion in each sign below).
- Assign one point if it is in the closest aspect to the Sun or Moon (conjunction, opposition, square, trine, or sextile, or semi-square (45 degrees) or sesquiquadrate (135 degrees); in regard to these last two aspects, the orb must be less than one degree.
- Assign one point if it is elevated in the chart.
- Assign one point if it is in its exalted sign.
- Assign one point if it is on its exaltation degree as follows:

  Sun at 18 degrees Aries 52 minutes
  Moon at 29 degrees Aries 17 minutes
  Mercury at 16 degrees Virgo 18 minutes
  Venus at 26 degrees Pisces 33 minutes
  Mars at 0 degrees Aquarius 48 minutes
  Jupiter at 15 degrees Cancer 14 minutes
  Saturn at 21 degrees Libra 9 minutes
- Assign one point if it is in aspect to another planetary body and it is in mutual reception with that other planetary body. Also assign one point to the other planetary body in that mutual reception. Mutual reception means planetary body A is in the sign ruled by the planetary body B in the aspect, and planetary body B is in the sign ruled by planetary body A in the aspect.
- Assign one point if the planet is Venus, Jupiter or Uranus. Subtract one point if the planet is Mars, Saturn, Neptune or Pluto.
- Assign one point to a planet if it is Venus, Jupiter or Uranus on the East point. The East point of the chart is the Ascendant of the chart if the race were held at the Equator.
- Assign one point to a planetary body if it is the natural ruler of the house in

which it is found. For example, Mercury is the natural ruler of the third house and the sixth house so if Mercury is located in either of these houses, assign one point to Mercury.

- Assign one point to a planetary body if it is conjunct a benefic fixed star (see the discussion below about fixed stars).
- Assign one point to a planetary body if it is on one of the following near midpoints in the chart: Ascendant/Midheaven, Midheaven/Descendant, Descendant/IC or IC/Ascendant. See the discussion below on how to get these midpoints.
- If a planet is retrograde, you can select it provided there are more than 2 days after its retrograde station date. If a planet is going retrograde, you can select it provided there are more than 2 days before its retrograde station date. If a planet just went direct, you can select it provided there are more than 2 days after its direct station date. If a planet is going direct, you can select it provided there are more than 2 days before its direct station date. To see the retrograde station dates and direct station dates of planets in a year, consult a good astrological calendar like Jim Maynard's Celestial Influences calendar.
- Don't bet a race if there is a solar eclipse or lunar eclipse on the date of the race unless you dare to.
- It is risky to use a planet that is in aspect to Neptune as Neptune is the planet of illusion and murky outcomes.
- If Neptune itself is in a trine aspect (120 degrees) to benefic planets like Jupiter, Venus and/or Uranus, and/or the lights (Sun and/or Moon), dreamy Neptune might actually come through with a big win, especially if Neptune is in Pisces, the sign that it rules.

Classical Lunar Mansion Degree Ranges

IN THE SIGN OF ARIES:

Zero degrees to 4 degrees 17 minutes is the lunar mansion of the Sun
4 degrees 17 minutes to 25 degrees 43 minutes is the lunar mansion of Venus
25 degrees 43 minutes to 29 degrees 59 minutes is the lunar mansion of Mercury

IN THE SIGN OF TAURUS:

Zero degrees to 4 degrees 17 minutes is the lunar mansion of the Moon
4 degrees 17 minutes to 25 degrees 43 minutes is the lunar mansion of Saturn
25 degrees 43 minutes to 29 degrees 59 minutes is the lunar mansion of Jupiter

IN THE SIGN OF GEMINI:

Zero degrees to 4 degrees 17 minutes is the lunar mansion of Jupiter
4 degrees 17 minutes to 25 degrees 43 minutes is the lunar mansion of Mars
25 degrees 43 minutes to 29 degrees 59 minutes is the lunar mansion of the Sun

IN THE SIGN OF CANCER:

Zero degrees to 4 degrees 17 minutes is the lunar mansion of the Sun
4 degrees 17 minutes to 25 degrees 43 minutes is the lunar mansion of Venus
25 degrees 43 minutes to 29 degrees 59 minutes is the lunar mansion of Mercury

IN THE SIGN OF LEO:

Zero degrees to 4 degrees 17 minutes is the lunar mansion of the Moon
4 degrees 17 minutes to 25 degrees 43 minutes is the lunar mansion of Saturn
25 degrees 43 minutes to 29 degrees 59 minutes is the lunar mansion of Jupiter

IN THE SIGN OF VIRGO:

Zero degrees to 4 degrees 17 minutes is the lunar mansion of Jupiter
4 degrees 17 minutes to 25 degrees 43 minutes is the lunar mansion of Mars
25 degrees 43 minutes to 29 degrees 59 minutes is the lunar mansion of the Sun

IN THE SIGN OF LIBRA:

Zero degrees to 4 degrees 17 minutes is the lunar mansion of the Sun
4 degrees 17 minutes to 25 degrees 43 minutes is the lunar mansion of Venus
25 degrees 43 minutes to 29 degrees 59 minutes is the lunar mansion of Mercury

IN THE SIGN OF SCORPIO:

Zero degrees to 4 degrees 17 minutes is the lunar mansion of the Moon
4 degrees 17 minutes to 25 degrees 43 minutes is the lunar mansion of Saturn
25 degrees 43 minutes to 29 degrees 59 minutes is the lunar mansion of Jupiter

IN THE SIGN OF SAGITTARIUS:
Zero degrees to 4 degrees 17 minutes is the lunar mansion of Jupiter
4 degrees 17 minutes to 25 degrees 43 minutes is the lunar mansion of Mars
25 degrees 43 minutes to 29 degrees 59 minutes is the lunar mansion of the Sun

IN THE SIGN OF CAPRICORN:
Zero degrees to 4 degrees 17 minutes is the lunar mansion of the Sun
4 degrees 17 minutes to 25 degrees 43 minutes is the lunar mansion of Venus
25 degrees 43 minutes to 29 degrees 59 minutes is the lunar mansion of Mercury

IN THE SIGN OF AQUARIUS:
Zero degrees to 4 degrees 17 minutes is the lunar mansion of the Moon
4 degrees 17 minutes to 25 degrees 43 minutes is the lunar mansion of Saturn
25 degrees 43 minutes to 29 degrees 59 minutes is the lunar mansion of Jupiter

IN THE SIGN OF PISCES:
Zero degrees to 4 degrees 17 minutes is the lunar mansion of Jupiter
4 degrees 17 minutes to 25 degrees 43 minutes is the lunar mansion of Mars
25 degrees 43 minutes to 29 degrees 59 minutes is the lunar mansion of the Sun

The importance of lunar mansions was presented by John Mazurek September 7, 1974 and can be read in its entirety on page 99 up to and including page 109 in the following:

> http://www.gramalkin.com/printable_versions/soulnars_sidereal_astrology.pdf

Fixed Stars

To see a list of the fixed stars that are conjunct planetary bodies in the chart of the race, you will need to create a chart of the race with Janus astrological software. Create the chart, open it and go to the Calculate dropdown at the top of the screen. Then select the Aspects to Stars selection to display the stars that are conjunct (at the same degree of) the planetary bodies in the chart. The meanings of these stars are also provided. Pick the planet that is conjunct the most favorable stars and assign one point to it. It's that simple.

Midpoints

Midpoints are exactly just that. For example Ascendant/Midheaven means the near midpoint between the Ascendant angle and the Midheaven angle in a chart. In the chart of the Santa Anita race below, the Ascendant is 26 degrees Aquarius 37 minutes. The Midheaven is 0 degrees Sagittarius 3 minutes. To find the near midpoint, convert 26 degrees Aquarius 37 minutes to degrees which is 326 degrees 37 minutes, and convert 0 degrees Sagittarius 3 minutes to degrees which is 240 degrees 3 minutes. Add them up (326 degrees 37 minutes plus 240 degrees 3 minutes) to arrive at 566 degrees 40 minutes. Divide 566 degrees 40 minutes by 2 to get 283 degrees 20 minutes and convert this to 13 degrees Capricorn 20 minutes.

Is there a planetary body on 13 degrees Capricorn 20 minutes in the chart? If so, assign one point to that planetary body.

To get the other three midpoints, follow this same procedure. If there are any planetary bodies on these midpoints, assign one point to them.

Chapter 4

THE RACE

The premier sources of horse racing information are the hardcopy and online Daily Racing Form (DRF) and the online Equibase of horse races. The DRF lists the entries in each race at several racetracks for a given day and it provides past performance data for each of these entries. The online version also displays the results of a race on the very same day of the race. The DRF is used to handicap i.e. figure out a race in advance using the analytics described in the information below. For a race, the horses are listed in the DRF in post position order, with the first post position at the top of the list until the last post position at the bottom of the list. Each listed horse has past performance data displayed with it.

Equibase provides the past performances and entries for horses on any track on any racing day. You can also research historical data using its powerful search engine. It has all the data on any horse or any race.

To sign up for the online DRF, visit www.drf.com or to buy the hardcopy DRF, visit your local newsstand. To get more information about the DRF and its various other publications, call 1-800-306-3676.

To sign up for Equibase, visit www.equibase.com. To get more information about Equibase, call 1-800-333-2211 or contact them at feedback@equibase.com.

In the DRF, each entry in a race contains the information shown on the next five pages, (Copyrighted c. 2016 by Daily Racing Form, LLC. Reprinted with Permission of the Copyright owner).

PAST PERFORMANCE EXPLANATION

Racing Daily Form DRF

Past Performance for display purposes only. *Daily Racing Form* exclusive feature highlighted in **Reverse Type**

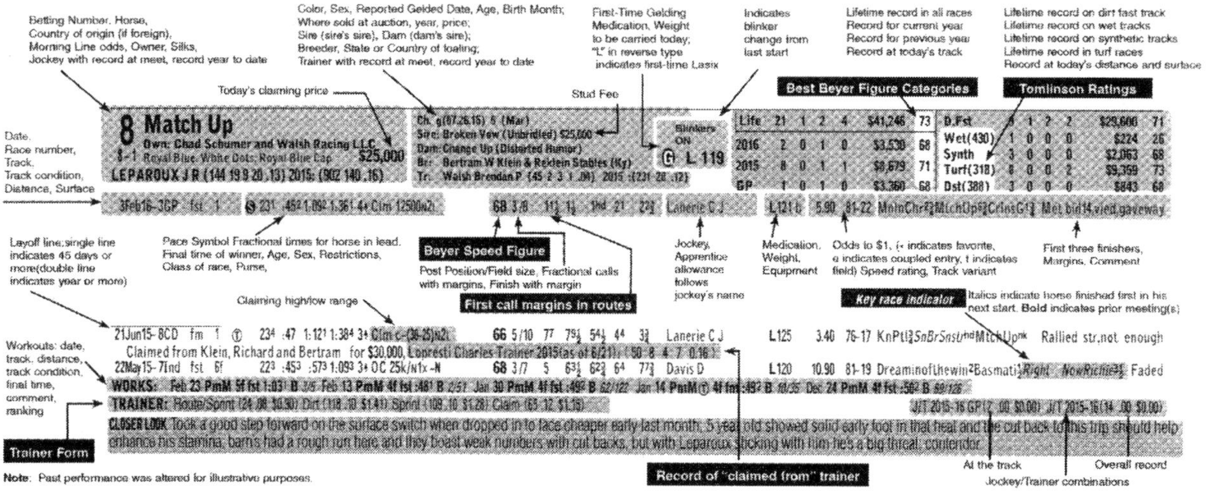

Note: Past performance was altered for illustrative purposes.

NEW PACE SYMBOLS

- Quickly identify race flows that favored a specific running style
- Easily find horses that may be better/worse than their PPs indicate

C - Favored **CLOSERS**
Ⓒ - Extremely Favored **CLOSERS**
S - Favored **SPEEDS**
Ⓢ - Extremely Favored **SPEEDS**

TRAINER FORM

Comprehensive Trainer Form Statistics: There are 36 trainer statistics that DRF is tracking, covering every trainer's record over this year and last year in a variety of situations. Up to 6 of these categories will show up under the bottom PP, depending on the number of applicable statistics.
Each trainer stat will list:

- the number of Starts for the trainer in this category,
- the Win Percentage for the trainer in this category
- and the $2.00 Return On Investment for the trainer in this category.

Category (12 0.17 $1.83)
Total Number of Starts — Winning percentage — Return on a $2 bet

BEYER SPEED FIGURES

Every performance by every horse in North America is assigned a Beyer Speed Figure that reflects the time of the race and the inherent speed of the track over which it was run, permitting easy comparisons of efforts at different distances and tracks. In this system, 2 1/2 points are roughly equal to one length in sprints and 2 points to one length in routes.

BEYER SCALE

115 +	The best horses in the country
100 + -	Good allowance horse or low-grade stakes horse
90 + -	A typical $25,000 claiming race
80 + -	A typical $10,000 claiming race
57 +-	Bottom level $2,500 claimers at smaller tracks

recent
l sales graduate

RACING POST RATINGS

Racing Post Ratings are a handicap rating determined by a horse's overall performance in a given race with respect to the race level, field quality, weight carried and time of the race. (Note: these are not directly comparable to speed ratings, which use different methodology).

Typical ratings for good winners

RACE	2YO	3YO	4YO+
Group 1	120	125	130
Group 2	115	117	120
Group 3	105	110	115
Listed race	95	105	110
Maiden	80	85	–

TOMLINSON RATINGS

Daily Racing Form past performances contain a special set of ratings called Tomlinson Ratings. These ratings appear in the career box above each horse's past performance. These three separate ratings (from 0 to 480) are based on a horse's breeding, and its likely aptitude for wet tracks, the turf, and compatibility with today's scheduled race distance. Distance ratings reflect all performances, regardless of whether races are run on dirt, turf or synthetic surfaces.
A wet rating of 320+ is a horse that merits further consideration on a muddy or sloppy track. The distance ratings, with a rating of 320 considered average, might prove especially useful when handicapping horses who may be better suited for sprints, middle distances or route races.
Tomlinson Ratings are especially useful in maiden races, 2-year-old races, races switched to a main track listed as "sloppy" or "muddy," horses trying mud, slop, or turf for the first or second time, or horses stretching out in distance.

SYMBOLS

[•]	Inner dirt track
[D]	Disqualified (symbol located next to odds and in company line)
[DH]	Dead-Heat (symbol located in company line if horses are among first three finishers)
♦	Dead-Heat (symbol used next to finish position)
3 ♦	Race for 3-year-olds and up
[S]	Race for state-breds only
[R]	Restricted race for horses who meet certain conditions
Ⓕ	Race for fillies, or fillies and mares
Ⓣ	Main turf course
[T]	Inner turf course
⊗	Race taken off turf
*	About distance
+	Start at infield chute
Ⓐ	All weather track
Ⓖ	First-time Gelding
	Recent Keeneland sales graduate

EQUIPMENT & MEDICATION

b	Blinkers
f	Front bandages
B	Butazolidin

TRACK CONDITIONS

DIRT TRACKS		TURF & STEEPLECHASE	
fst	Fast		
wf	Wet-Fast	hd	Hard
gd	Good	fm	Firm
sly	Sloppy	gd	Good
my	Muddy	yl	Yielding
sl	Slow	sf	Soft
hy	Heavy	hy	Heavy
fr	Frozen		

WORKOUT LINE

z	Best of day/distance
B	Breezing
D	Driving
(d)	Worked around dogs
E	Easily
g	Worked from gate
H	Handily
tr.t	Training track
TR	Training race
3/25	Workout ranking
(W)	Wood Chips
Ⓐ	All weather track

ABBREVIATIONS FOR TYPES OF RACES

Alw 15000N1X	Non-winners of one race (or more, depending on the number after N) other than maiden, claiming or starter. Used for non-winners of up to 5 races "other than"
Alw 15000N1Y	Non-winners of one race (or more, depending on the number after N) in, or since, a specified time period
Alw 15000N2L	Non-winners of two (or more, depending on the number after N) races lifetime
Alw 15000N$Y	Non-winners of a specific amount of money in a specified time period
Alw 15000N1m	Non-winners of one (or more, depending on the number after N) races at a mile or over in a specified time period
Alw 15000N$mY	Non-winners of a specific amount of money OR races at a mile or over in, or since, a specified time period
Alw 15000N1s	Non-winners of one (or more) stakes lifetime
Alw 15000N1T	Non-winners of one (or more) turf races
Alw 15000NmT	Non-winners of one or more turf races at a mile or more
Alw 150000NC	Allowance race with no conditions
Alw 15000c	Allowance race with multiple conditions or restrictions
Alw 15000s	Starter allowance (number indicates minimum claiming price horse must have started for to be eligible)
CLM (10-9)	Claiming race (entered to be claimed for $10,000)
Clm 10-9000N2L	Non-winners of two races (or more, depending on the number after n) lifetime
Clm 10-9000N2x	Non-winners of two races (or more, depending on the number after n) other than those described in the conditions of a race.
Clm 10-9000N1Y	Non-winners of one race (or more) in, or since, a specified time period.
Clm10-9000N1mY	Non-winners of one race (or more) at a mile or over in, or since, a specified time period
Clm10-9000N$Y	Non-winners of a specific amount of money in, or since, a specified time period
Clm10-9000N$mY	Non-winners of a specific amount of money OR races at a mile or over in, or since, a specified time period
Clm10-9000B	Claiming race with multiple conditions or restrictions
Clm Stk 10000	Claiming stakes (number indicates claiming price)
OC 40k/n2x-N	Optional claiming race with allowance condition Entered NOT to be claimed
Hcp 10000s	Starter handicap race. Number indicates minimum claiming price horse must have started for to be eligible

OTHER CONDITIONS

Md Sp Wt 8k	Maiden Special Weight race (for non-winners), purse value
Moc 40000	Maiden Optional Claiming race
Md 32000 (32-30)	Maiden Claiming race (entered to be claimed for $32,000)
Handicap 40k	Overnight handicap race (purse of $40,000)
Ky Derby-G1	Graded Stakes race, with name of race (North American races are graded in order of status, with G1 being the best)
PrincetonH 40k	Ungraded, but named Stakes race (H indicates handicap) Purse value is $40,000

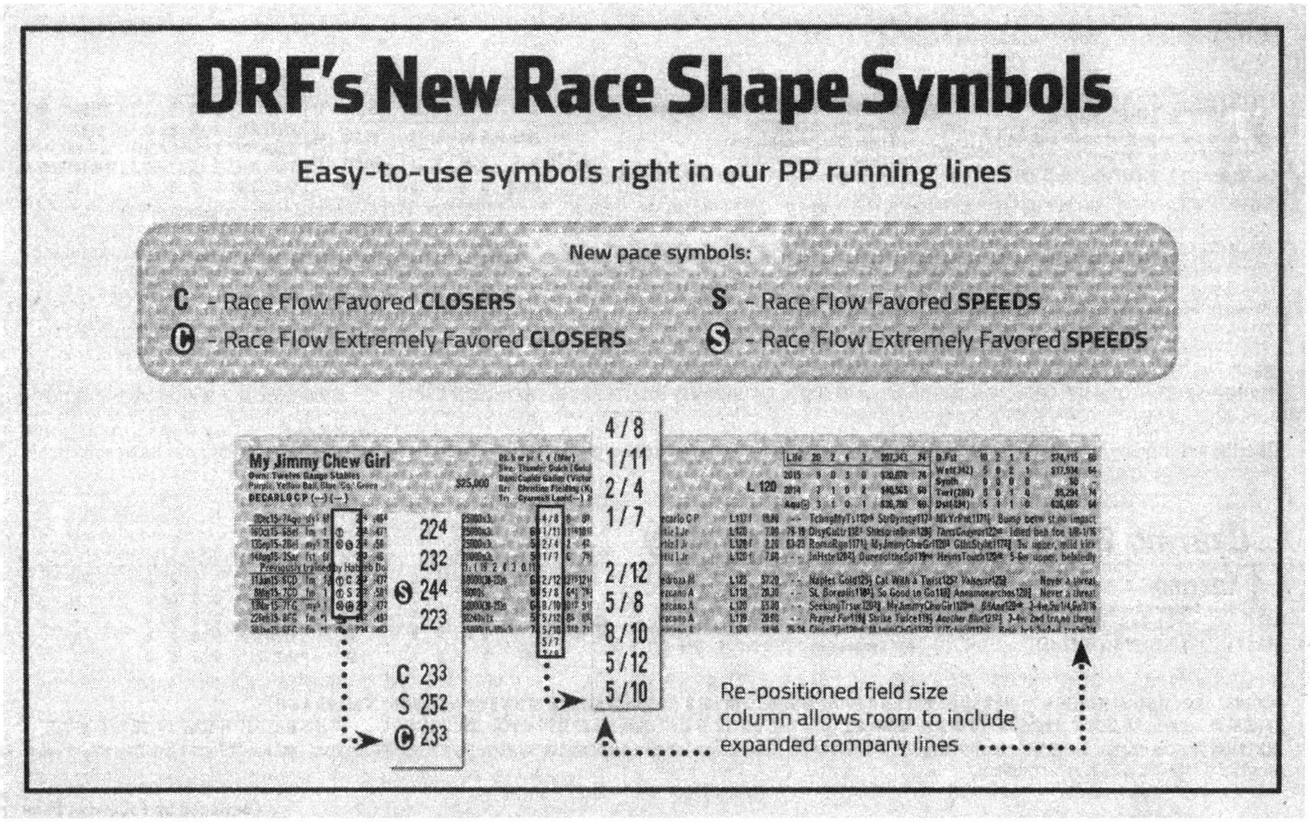

Here is a brief glossary of a sample entry from the online Daily Racing Form: From:

http://www1.drf.com/help/help_drf_pp.html

Data in a Past Performance

There is a tremendous amount of data available for interpretation in a DRF past performance. Below, you'll see a sample past performance (PP). This list will help you identify what each piece of data means, including six new features from DRF: Tomlinson Ratings, New Class Codes, Next Out Winners Italicized in Company Lines, Stud Fees, Bar Shoes, ad The Career Box.

The following data elements are in a Daily Racing Form Past Performance (* - new features):

Tomlinson Ratings Tomlinson Ratings, which appear next to the "Turf" and "Wet" headings in each horse's career box, measure a horses potential to handle turf and muddy/sloppy track conditions. Previous Trainer Line - This indicates horse's previous trainer.

Date Race was Run 1Jan96. This race was run on Jan 1, 1996.

Race Number, Track 10CRC. This was the tenth race at Calder. A complete list of track abbreviations is published in the past performance section of most issues of Daily Racing Form. A diamond symbol preceding a track name denotes a foreign racetrack.

Track Condition gd. The track was good.

Distance of Race 5 furlongs. This race was at 5 furlongs on the main dirt track. An asterisk (*) before the distance indicates it was an approximate, or "about," distance (*7f = about 7 furlongs).

Fractional Times :22 :46.1. Three fractional times are given for each race at all distances over 5 1/2 furlongs. In this 5 furlong race, the first fraction (:22) is the leader's time after a quarter-mile; the second fraction (:46.1) is the leader's time after a half-mile.

Final Time :59.2. The winning horse stopped the teletimer in :59.2. This is always the time of the first horse to cross the finish line, even if the winner is disqualified from first position.

Type of Race Alw 18700N1X. This was an allowance race for non-winners of a race other than maiden or claiming.

****New Class Codes*** In claiming races the range of claiming prices is noted - 16/14000.

Beyer Speed Figure 53. Beyer Speed Figures are available exclusively in Daily Racing Form. Every performance by every horse in North America is assigned a number which reflects the time of the race and the inherent speed of the track over which it was run, and permits easy comparison of efforts at different distances. A figure of 95 denotes exactly the same quality of performance whether is was earned at Santa Anita or Suffolk Downs.

Post Position 6. The horse left the starting gate from stall number six. Post position can differ from official program number because of late scratches, horses coupled as a betting entry, or runners grouped in a mutuel field.

First Call 9. The horse's position immediately after leaving the starting gate or after quarter-mile depending on the distance. This horse was ninth after the start.

Second Call 10-9 1/2. This horse was tenth, 9 1/2 lengths behind the leader after three-sixteenths of a mile. The large figure indicates the horse's running position, the smaller figure is the margin behind the leader. If the horse had been in front at this point the smaller figure would indicate the margin in front of the second horse.

Third Call 9-14. The horse was ninth, 14 lengths behind the leader after three-eighths of a mile.

Stretch Call 9-14. The horse was ninth, 14 lengths behind the leader at this point. The stretch call is always made one furlong (one-eighth of a mile) from the finish line.

Finish 9-10 3/4. The horse finished 9th, 10 3/4 lengths behind the winner. If the horse was the winner, the smaller figure would indicate the margin ahead of the second horse. A symbol after the finish means the horse finished in a deadheat with one or more horses for that position.

Jockey Davis RG. This horse was ridden by Robbie Davis. When a small number follows the jockey's name it indicates the apprentice allowance claimed. Apprentice riders are entitled to weight allowances of 3, 5, 7 or 10 pounds, based on experience and contract rules. Daily Racing Form publishes complete jockey/trainer standings for every track several times each week.

Medication L, B. Where state rules permit, horses may run on various medications. L indicates a horse has been treated with Lasix (generic name: furosemide); B indicates horse has been treated with Butazolidin (generic name: phenylbutazone).

L lasix. The L1 indicates first time lasix.

Weight Carried 119. The horse carried 119 pounds in this race. This is the weight of the rider and equipment (saddle, lead pads, etc.) and includes the apprentice allowance when an allowance is claimed.

Blinkers On or Off. This indicates blinker changes from last start

Equipment f The letter "f" indicates the horse wore front bandages. If the horse wore blinkers, the letter b would appear after the f (fb).

***Bar Shoes** r The letter "r" indicates the horse wore bar shoes.

Closing Odds 41.00. The horse was $41.00 to the dollar. The * symbol preceding the odds indicates the horse was the betting favorite. The letter "e" following the odds means the horse was coupled in the betting (an entry) with one or more horse. The letter "f" in this position would indicate the horse was in the mutuel field.

Speed Rating, Track Variant 81-18. The first number is the speed rating, a comparison of this horse's time with the best time at the distance at that track in the last three years, which is represented by the par value of 100. The second figure (18) is the track variant, which shows how many points below par the times for all races at the distance on the same surface were that day. See the Speed Rating/Track Variant page for detailed explanation.

First Three Horses at Finish Outlaw Sweetie 119 1/2, Family Influence 119 hd, Devils Reality 119 2 1/2. The "company line" shows the horses which finished first, second and third in the race, the weight each carried and the margins separating each one from the next horse.

***Next Out Winners Italicized in Company Lines** Names printed in bold face type are also entered in today's race. Horses italicized won their next start.

Comment Line Outrun. A capsule description of the horse's performance written by the chart caller, with special emphasis on pointing out any trouble encountered.

Number of Starters 10. Ten horses started in this race.

Workouts Latest workouts are printed under each horse's past performances. Daily Racing Form carries up to six works for all horses, with up to 12 for first-time starters. The bullet indicates this was the best workout of the day at that track and distance. Workouts are ranked by the numbers in italics (1/10). Another example would be the December 24 workout at Calder. Gina's Angel worked six furlongs in 1:14.4 seconds (4/20), the fourth-best workout of the 20 horses that went six furlongs that morning.

***Career Box** Indicates lifetime, current year, prior year and record at track on left side. Indicates dirt, wet, turf and record at distance on right side. Beyer figures following these lines indicate best Beyer Speed Figure on dirt fast tracks (58), wet tracks (73), turf (53) and today's distance and surface (22).

Pedigree Information Top line indicates color, sex, age and month fooled. Second line indicates sire, sire's sire followed by *sire's stud fee if available. Third line indicates breeder and state bred.

Owner/Trainer/Jockey This information appears above the past performances. The record of the jockey at the current meeting and for the current year appears after his/her name. The same information follows the trainer's name.

To receive a free guide to Daily Racing Form past performances, send your name and mailing address via e-mail to cservice@drf.com.

In the past performances of a horse, if you see that the horse was scratched before the present race and a small 'v' appears in that information, a veterinarian decided the horse had to be scratched. Chances are the medical condition was corrected. This horse will probably run well in the present race.

The following sources can also be used to understand how to support your pick:

- *Handicapping 101* by Brad Free available from the DRF for $14.95. An excellent primer on the basics of horse-racing.
- *Betting on Horse Racing for Dummies* by Richard Eng. Don't let the title fool you. This is an excellent book.
- *Cashing Big on Racing's Biggest Days* by Steve Davidowitz published by the DRF. A good book for betting on big racing days.
- www.todaysracingdigest.com which also provides the services of expert handicappers at several racetracks.
- www.runhorse.com/list_of_world_thoroughbred_horse_racing_tracks.htm for information on the world's thoroughbred horse racetracks.
- www.thoroughbredracingworld.com
- www.helloracefans.com
- www.horseracingnation.com
- www.equineline.com

- www.horse-races.net
- www.gallop-magazine.com
- www.americanturf.com

On race day, don't forget to note the track conditions of the race: is the track sloppy from rain, does your horse like to run on a muddy track, is it a fast dry track, do you think the turf in a turf race is firm (from no rain) or soft (from rain), will they take the horses off the wet, soft turf and put them on a muddy track? On a muddy track, mud will be flung in the faces of horses that don't break well out of the starting gate. Your horse will have to deal with these conditions.

To get the latest conditions one half hour before the race, you can call HPI Bets at 1-888-675-8886 for personalized service. For automated service, you can call 1-888-675-6337 or 1-416-623-6337. When you call automated service, you will be asked for an access code which is actually a race track code (you can type 12 followed by # to access Belmont). Then when prompted, hit # again to hear a list of racetracks and codes from which you can get the racetrack code of the racetrack you want. Then type in that code followed by # to get the conditions for the card at that racetrack. Of course, you can also get the latest conditions by being at the racetrack.

Using www.bloodhorse.com you can view the male parent (stallion) sire of the horse and the female parent (mare) dam of the horse to see if the breeding affects the short range speed or long range endurance of your horse.

Don't forget you are betting against other bettors, not the house, so you have a really good chance to win!

Chapter 5

CHART OF THE RACE

To create the chart of the race, bring up Solar Fire and enter the place, date, place and post time of the race to create the chart. On the next page is the chart of a race in Solar Fire.

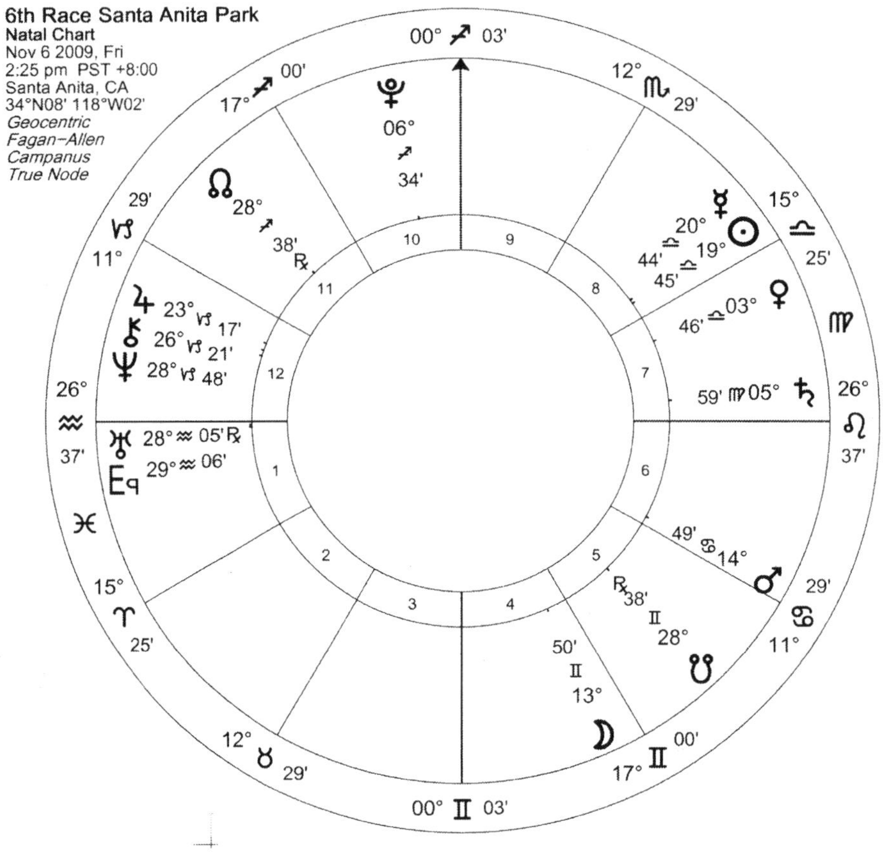

The horse Midday at post position 6 is Venus in the sign it rules (Libra) for 2 points, is in the house that it naturally rules (the seventh for 1 point), is elevated in the chart (1 point) and it is Venus the benefic for 1 point for a total of 5 points. Magical Fantasy at post position 4 is Uranus on the Ascendant angle for 2 points and is in its ruling sign Aquarius for 2 points for the total of 4 points, and Uranus is in exact aspect to Neptune at 28 degrees which could deny success for Uranus hence Magical Fantasy. According to the fixed stars analysis in Janus "Neptune is conjunct Deneb Algedi (in Capricorn) in the 'tail of the goat.' Associated with the positive aspects of Jupiter and Saturn, this star confers a sense of justice and integrity, with the gaining of others' confidence or the attaining of positions of trust such as a counsellor or advisor. *Fluctuating fortunes are also possible.* Neptune is also conjunct Sadalsuud meaning 'luckiest of the lucky,' in Arabic. However its influence is said to bring trouble and disgrace. Nature of Mercury and Saturn." I went with Venus which had 5 points as the most powerful planetary body in the chart. Venus represented Midday the winner of the race.

On the next four pages are the past performances of the horses in the race and the results of the race provided by the DRF, (Copyrighted © 2016 by Daily Racing Form, LLC. Reprinted with Permission of the Copyright owner).

Daily Racing Form ***20160616. Santa Anita. 1 1/4 Miles. Turf. Thoroughbred***

Visit (GB)

Own: Juddmonte Farms Inc

Dk. b or b. f. 4 (May)
Sire: Oasis Dream*GB (Green Desert)
Dam: Arrive*GB (Kahyasi*Ire)
Br: Juddmonte Farms Ltd (GB)
Tr: Frankel Robert J(0 0 0 0 .00) 2009:(0 0 .00)

Life	16	2	4	4	$646,856	102	D.Fst	0	0	0	0	$0	-
2009	7	0	2	1	$186,472	98	Wet(235*)	0	0	0	0	$0	-
							Synth	1	0	0	0	$0	83
2008	5	1	1	3	$410,526	102	Turf(390)	15	2	4	4	$646,856	102
Sa Ⓣ	3	0	1	2	$291,000	102	DstⓉ(323)	2	0	1	1	$273,000	102

10Oct09-4OSA	fm	1¼ Ⓣ	472 1:114 1:36 1:592	3↑ⒻYlwRibbn-G1	98	7/8	21	21	21	1½	2½	Gomez G K	LB123	3.70	87-08	Magical Fantasy½ Visitno *Black Mamba*1½	Led into str,edged
16Aug09-8Dmr	fm	1⅛ Ⓣ	48 1:12 1:353 1:47	3↑ⒻJCMabee-G1	95	8/9	84¾	84¾	85	65	42	Blanc B	LB119	5.00	86-12	*MagicalFantasy*1 *GottaHaveHer*½ PatricisGem½	5wd into str,missed 3d
11Jly09-10Hol	fm	1 Ⓣ	234 :471 1:104 1:333	3↑ⒻRlHrinMl-G2	94	8/8	77	74¾	63¼	63¼	42	Blanc B	LB119	3.40	94-07	TuscanEveningno PatriciasGem1¾ GottHveHernk	3wd into str,missed 3d
30May09-9Hol	fm	1⅛ Ⓣ	483 1:121 1:36 1:48	+3↑ⒻGamely-G1	98	4/9	52½	52½	42½	31	2nk	Blanc B	LB117	10.20	81-18	*Magical Fantasy*nk Visitno Diamond Diva1½	Bid,btwn late,game
2May09-8CD	gd	1 Ⓣ	243 :491 1:143 1:384	3↑ⒻDstfTfMl-G2	81	2/9	85½	87	84¾	64½	54¼	Gomez G K	L118	*1.50	72-22	Tizaqueena¾ Dawn After Dawn½ Lemon Chiffon2	Squeezed, steadied
22Mar09-8SA	gd	1⅛ Ⓣ	481 1:123 1:364 1:483	4↑ⒻSntaAnaH-G2	87	5/7	64	53½	53	41¾	3nk	Gomez G K	LB118	*.70	85-15	Belmont Cathd Bel Air Sizzlenk Visithd	Angled out,closed btwn
14Feb09-9SA	fst	1 1/16 ◈	233 :472 1:112 1:414	4↑ⒻSntMriaH-G1	83	6/8	87½	85¾	84¾	76¼	611¼	Gomez G K	LB118	*1.50	77-12	Santa Teresita2½ DHModel1¼ DHMarzelline1¼	Pulled early,no bid
30Nov08-7Hol	fm	1 Ⓣ	253 :49 1:12 1:352	3↑ⒻMatriarc-G1	93	6/8	75	74¾	74½	74¾	31¼	Gomez G K	LB120	3.40	86-13	Cocoa Beach¾ Precious Kitten½ Visit¾	Pulled early,rallied
Previously trained by Stoute Sir Michael 2008(as of 10/24): (1 0 0 1 0.00)																	
24Oct08-6OSA	fm	1¼ Ⓣ	50 1:143 1:38 2:012	3↑ⒻBCFMTrf-G1	102	4/10	86	85½	63½	1hd	41½	Moore R L	B118	17.80	82-11	*Forever Together*¾ Sealy Hillhd DWait a While¾	Rail bid,led,outkicked
Awarded third purse money																	

4Oct08 Newmarket (GB)	gf	1	Ⓣ Str 1:352	3↑ ⒻSun Chariot Stakes-G1	Stk 378000	10	31½	Munro A	125	20.00	Halfway To Heaven½ Darjina1 Visit3¾	Tracked leaders,angled right over 1f out,stayed on.Nahoodh7th
Racing Post Rating: 114												
1Aug08 Goodwood (GB)	gf	7f	Ⓣ RH 1:26	3↑ ⒻOak Tree Stakes-G3	Stk 138800	14	1hd	Moore R L	121	*2.00	Visithd Cheyenne Star2¼ *Shabiba*nk	Rated in 8th,progress into 2nd 1-1/2f out,led 1f out,held gamely
Racing Post Rating: 108												
5Jly08 Sandown Park (GB)	gf	1	Ⓣ RH 1:414	ⒻDistaff Stakes (Listed)	Stk 79300	11	2nk	Moore R L	130	6.00	Rosaleennk *Visit*¾ Illusion1	Rated in 7th,progress 2f out,2nd 75y out,gaining late
Racing Post Rating: 104+												
5Oct07 Newmarket (GB)	gd	6f	Ⓣ Str 1:112	ⒻCheveley Park Stakes-G1	Stk 368000	14	86¾	Moore R L	124	*2.75	*Natagora*nk *Fleeting Spirit*4 Festoso1	Rated towards rear,brief progress 2f out,failed to threaten
Racing Post Rating: 96												
23Aug07 York (GB)	gd	6f	Ⓣ Str 1:123	ⒻLowther Stakes-G2	Stk 169000	10	2½	Moore R L	124	*1.50	Nahoodh½ DVisit¾ *Fleeting Spirit*no	Tracked in 3rd,lacked room 2f out,gamely.DQ'd,drug positive
Racing Post Rating: 104												
Disqualified and placed 10th												
29Jly07 Ascot (GB)	gs	6f	Ⓣ Str 1:164	ⒻPrincess Margaret Stakes-G3	Stk 81000	13	11½	Moore R L	124	*3.30	Visit1½ Reel Gift2½ Sweepstakenk	Slowly away,soon mid-pack,drifted right & led 170y out,driving
Racing Post Rating: 107												
29Jun07 Newmarket (GB)	gs	6f	Ⓣ Str 1:142	ⒻJuly Course Series EBF Maiden Stakes	Maiden 20000	12	2hd	Moore R L	126	8.00	Don't Forget Faithhd *Visit*1½ Honky Tonk Sally1¾	Trckd in 4th,angled right over 1f out,fnshd well.LadyDeauville5th
Racing Post Rating: 85+												

Forever Together

Own: Augustin Stable

Gr/ro. m. 5 (Apr)
Sire: Belong to Me (Danzig) $10,000
Dam: Constant Companion (Relaunch)
Br: White Fox Farm (Ky)
Tr: Sheppard Jonathan E(0 0 0 0 .00) 2009:(0 0 .00)

Life	19	9	3	4	$2,604,639	105	D.Fst	7	3	0	1	$153,140	93
2009	5	2	2	1	$600,106	101	Wet(391)	0	0	0	0	$0	-
							Synth	1	0	1	0	$50,000	82
2008	7	4	0	2	$1,803,993	105	Turf(330)	11	6	2	3	$2,407,360	105
Sa Ⓣ	1	1	0	0	$1,150,200	105	DstⓉ(305)	1	1	0	0	$1,150,200	105

10Oct09-7Kee	sf	1 Ⓣ	241 :48 1:124 1:383	3↑ⒻFstLdy-G1	100	5/9	815	920	917	58½	31½	Leparoux J R	L123	*1.10	75-23	Diamondrella¾ Tizaqueena¾ Forever Together½	4 wide,closed fast
20Sep09-4WO	fm	*1⅛ Ⓣ	482	1:45 3↑ⒻCanadian-G2	97	5/7	45	53½	55	3½	2no	Leparoux J R	L124	*.30	102 -	PrincessHyno ForeverTogetherhd *MuchObligd*2	Bid furlong out,missed
1Aug09-9Sar	gd	1⅛ Ⓣ	482 1:122 1:362 1:481	3↑ⒻDiana-G1	101	10/10	98½	98	87½	32	1hd	Leparoux J R	L123	*.95	85-14	Forever Togetherhd Carribean Sunset¾ Rutherienne1½	4wide, prevailed
6Jun09-7Bel	yl	1 Ⓣ	234 :474 1:121 1:362	3↑ⒻJsAGm-G1	101	4/7	64½	64½	62	2hd	21¾	Leparoux J R	L123	*.70	76-21	Dimondrell1¾ *ForeverTogether*1¼ MyPrincessJss½	Blocked turn, rallied
11Apr09-8Kee	gd	1 1/16 Ⓣ	254 :514 1:17 1:464	4↑ⒻJenyWily-G2	99	3/7	64½	64½	61¾	1hd	11	Leparoux J R	L123	*1.00	69-25	Forever Together1 *Rutherienne*nk Kiss With a Twist3¼	Ridden out
24Oct08-6OSA	fm	1¼ Ⓣ	50 1:143 1:38 2:012	3↑ⒻBCFMTrf-G1	105	3/10	75	74	75	83½	1¾	Leparoux J R	LB123	4.90	84-11	*Forever Together*¾ Sealy Hillhd DWait a While¾	5wd into lane,rallied
3Oct08-8Kee	fm	1 Ⓣ	234 :474 1:111 1:35	3↑ⒻFstLdy-G1	104	6/7	64	54	52½	22½	11½	Leparoux J R	L123	2.50	95 -	*ForeverTogether*1½ PreciousKitten2 Rutherienn½	Waited briefly 1/4 pl
7Sep08-4WO	yl	1⅛ Ⓣ	494 1:14 1:384 1:514	3↑ⒻCanadian-G2	95	3/11	106½	118	107½	52½	33	Leparoux J R	L124	*.80	71-21	J'ray1 Callwood Dancer2 *Forever Together*2¾	Gamely rail,evn'd out
26Jly08-7Sar	gd	1⅛ Ⓣ	464 1:104 1:343 1:462	3↑ⒻDiana-G1	105	8/10	1010	1015	99½	73½	1¾	Leparoux J R	L118	9.00	94-06	Forever Together¾ Dynaforce3½ Rutherienneno	Going away
7Jun08-7Bel	fm	1 Ⓣ	232 :462 1:093 1:323	3↑ⒻJsAGm-G1	101	6/10	1010	108½	96	63½	31½	Dominguez R A	L118	44.00	95-09	Ventura¾ Lady of Venice¾ *Forever Together*nk	Steadied turn
17May08-9AP	yl	1 Ⓣ	252 :50 1:143 1:39	3↑ⒻRluctntGst53k	87	5/9	77½	63½	62½	4nk	11¼	Fires E	L118	8.10	83-21	ForeverTogether1¼ *Lemonlime*no *LadyLionel*1	Ran down leaders 5wide
15Feb08-5GP	fst	7f	222 :45 1:091 1:222	4↑ⒻOC 75k/N3X-N	78	5/7	1	42½	34	34	43¾	Trujillo E	L120	1.80	89-07	Featherbed1¼ Casa Mimaty1 Girls Pearls1½	No response
29Dec07-8Crc	fst	7f	213 :442 1:10 1:241	3↑ⒻChapSprngH100k	66	3/7	6	45½	47	59½	59¾	Trujillo E	L119	3.00	82-12	Cher Ami5¾ *Change Up*1¼ Running Lass1½	Failed to menace
24Nov07-10Crc	fst	7f	222 :452 1:104 1:242	3↑ⒻConnieAnn35k	85	4/7	3	64½	55½	33	32¼	Trujillo E	L118	*1.20	89-09	RunningLass2¼ *AmazingSpeed*hd ForeverTogether2¼	Finished willingly
16Jun07-8Del	fst	1 1/16	232 :471 1:113 1:424	ⒻSusanGrlBC180k	69	6/7	32	31	31	610	615¼	Pino M G	L116	1.40	86-11	*Moon Catcher*2 Winning Point2 Greenstreet2	Stalked pace, empty
12Apr07-8Kee	fst	*7f ◈	231 :452 1:09 1:244	ⒻBeaumont-G2	82	5/7	4	42	42¾	32½	2nk	Velasquez C	L121	*1.50	97-05	*Street Sounds*nk Forever Together1¾ Palace Pier2½	5w,couldn't get up
10Mar07-7GP	fst	7f	221 :451 1:093 1:223	ⒻFrwrdGal-G2	93	6/7	2	21½	21	11½	12	Trujillo E	L118	5.10	92-13	ForeverTogether2 SilverKnockrs3¾ YouAskdno	Bobbled st, edged away
12Feb07-10TC	fst	6f	222 :45 :573 1:102	ⒻⓇOBSSprint50k	86	2/8	4	52	33	21	12½	Trujillo E	120	-	98-01	*Forever Together*2½ Taletobetold3 *Lia's Luck*6¼	Split h,ran past leadr
Non-wagering event																	
5Nov06-5Del	fst	6f	224 :464 :591 1:111	ⒻMd Sp Wt 40k	79	8/8	3	1hd	11½	12	13¼	Pino M G	121	4.50	85-16	*Forever Together*3¼ *All Night Labor*4 Diamondbreaker6½	Ridden out

Rutherienne

Own: Virginia Kraft Payson LLC

Dk. b or b. m. 5 (Feb)
Sire: Pulpit (A.P. Indy) $80,000
Dam: Ruthian (Rahy)
Br: Payson Stud, Inc. (Ky)
Tr: Clement Christophe(0 0 0 0 .00) 2009:(0 0 .00)

Life	22	11	2	7	$1,280,671	101	D.Fst	0	0	0	0	$0	-
2009	5	2	2	1	$359,116	99	Wet(388)	0	0	0	0	$0	-
							Synth	0	0	0	0	$0	-
2008	7	1	0	6	$300,580	101	Turf(329)	22	11	2	7	$1,295,755	101
Sa Ⓣ	0	0	0	0	$0	-	DstⓉ(316)	0	0	0	0	$0	-

19Sep09-4Bel	fm	1 Ⓣ	223 :47 1:12 1:341	3↑ⒻNblDmslH-G3	98	7/7	612	53½	52½	2hd	1no	Garcia Alan	L123	*.40	89-10	Rutherienneno Quiet Meadow3½ Social Queen½	Up final jump
29Aug09-9Sar	sf	1 1/16 Ⓣ	254 :514 1:171 1:471	3↑ⒻBlstSpaH-G2	98	1/7	53½	54	63½	1hd	2hd	Garcia Alan	L120	*1.85	62-38	Salve Germaniahd *Rutherienne*½ My Princess Jess¾	Split, led, caught
1Aug09-9Sar	gd	1⅛ Ⓣ	482 1:122 1:362 1:481	3↑ⒻDiana-G1	99	3/10	54	53½	53½	63	3¾	Garcia Alan	L120	4.70	84-14	ForeverTogetherhd CrribenSunset¾ Rutherinn1½	Steadied, no room str
30May09-8WO	gd	1 1/16 Ⓣ	243 :482 1:121 1:414	3↑ⒻNassau-G2	98	5/9	42½	31½	31½	1½	13	Garcia Alan	L119	*.80	87-13	Rutherienne3 CallwoodDncer¾ *MedowSffron*¾	Hemmed in,up 1/8pl,drv
11Apr09-8Kee	gd	1 1/16 Ⓣ	254 :514 1:17 1:464	4↑ⒻJenyWily-G2	97	7/7	52½	53	51¾	2hd	21	Garcia Alan	L117	5.90	68-25	ForeverTogether1 *Rutherienn*nk KissWithTwist3¼	Bumped midstretch
6Dec08-8Crc	fm	1⅛ Ⓣ	482 1:114 1:353 1:473	3↑ⒻMyChrmrH-G3	100	8/12	85¾	74	83¼	44	31¼	Douglas R R	L121	*1.30	90-17	*WildPromises*1 CallwoodDncernk Rutheriennenk	Out lane,outfnshd 2nd
3Oct08-8Kee	fm	1 Ⓣ	234 :474 1:111 1:35	3↑ⒻFstLdy-G1	97	3/7	54	64	63	44½	33½	Gomez G K	L123	4.20	91 -	*Forever Together*1½ Precious Kitten2 Rutherienne½	Bmpd st, rail to str
21Aug08-8Sar	fm	1 1/16 Ⓣ	234 :47 1:101 1:393	3↑ⒻBlstSpaH-G2	100	4/5	57	58	46½	32	32¼	Leparoux J R	L119	3.05	99 -	*Wait a While*1 *Carriage Trail*1½ Rutherienne2¾	Rail move, split 1/8pl
26Jly08-7Sar	gd	1⅛ Ⓣ	464 1:104 1:343 1:462	3↑ⒻDiana-G1	98	7/10	99½	914	1011	97	34¼	Gomez G K	L120	6.10	90-06	Forever Together¾ Dynaforce3½ Rutherienneno	Rail trip, angled out
21Jun08-8Cnl	gd	1⅛ Ⓣ	484 1:14 1:393 1:52	3↑ⒻAlAlngBC-G3	92	7/7	69½	610	75¾	42½	32¾	Gomez G K	L122	*.70	69-28	Lady Digby2¼ Eclisse½ Rutherienne½	Off rail,run btw 1/16
26May08-3Hol	fm	1⅛ Ⓣ	454 1:084 1:331 1:451	+3↑ⒻGamely-G1	101	4/5	34	37	36	34	33¾	Nakatani C S	LB123	2.30	91-09	Precious Kitten2¼ *Diamond Diva*1½ Rutherienne3¼	Pulled bit,best rest
12Apr08-6Kee	fm	1 1/16 Ⓣ	251 :502 1:151 1:443	4↑ⒻJenyWily-G2	95	4/10	95¾	96	83¾	41½	1nk	Gomez G K	L119	6.00	79-14	Rutheriennenk Stormy Westhd Lady of Venicehd	Split 4w,stiff drive
29Dec07-11Crc	fm	7½f Ⓣ	23 :454 1:10 1:28	ⒻFAGenter-G3	90	7/11	8	65	64¾	2½	1nk	Douglas R R	L121	*1.30	94-04	*Rutherienne*nk DHSweet Ransom1½ DHPretoria Light1½	Rallied, up late
8Sep07-7Bel	fm	1⅛ Ⓣ	501 1:142 1:374 1:484	ⒻGrdnCy-G1	80	10/10	74½	82½	82½	105	105½	Gomez G K	L122	*1.60	75-12	Alexander Tango¾ *Bit of Whimsy*no Sharp Susanno	Wide trip, tired
18Aug07-8Dmr	fm	1⅛ Ⓣ	462 1:102 1:35 1:463	ⒻDMrOaks-G1	98	8/10	98½	97½	85½	41½	12	Nakatani C S	LB122	3.60	90-10	Rutherienne2 Valbenny4½ Super Freakynk	5wd into lane,rallied
27Jly07-8Sar	fm	1 1/16 Ⓣ	23 :464 1:103 1:401	ⒻLkGeorge-G3	94	10/11	914	99½	95½	21½	1nk	Gomez G K	L122	*2.75	96-04	*Rutherienne*nk Lady Attacknk *Sharp Susan*1	Got through on hedge
30Jun07-9Mth	fm	1 1/16 Ⓣ	241 :474 1:104 1:403	+ⒻBlngSpg-G3	93	1/6	53½	55	54	31	2nk	Bravo J	L118	*.80	96-08	DRed Birkinnk *Rutherienne*1¼ Sharp Susan3½	Eased out,bumped late
Placed first through disqualification																	
2Jun07-8Bel	fm	1⅛ Ⓣ	492 1:14 1:364 1:482	ⒻSandsPnt-G3	92	4/6	63½	63½	52½	42½	1½	♦Gomez G K	L121	*1.45	83-17	DH*Rutherienne*½ DHBit of Whimsy½ Classic Neel2½	Fast finish outside
12May07-3Bel	fm	1 1/16 Ⓣ	25 :492 1:132 1:43	ⒻSgrPlmTime68k	89	2/7	73¾	72¼	41¼	21	11¾	Gomez G K	L118	*.75	78-22	*Rutherienne*1¾ *Silence Dogood*¾ Olivine½	3 wide move, clear
22Apr07-8Kee	fm	1 Ⓣ	242 :484 1:133 1:361	ⒻApplachian115k	84	5/12	115½	119	104	86¼	41½	Gomez G K	L121	6.70	84-12	*Audacious Chloe*nk Classic Neelnk *Red Birkin*1	6w lane,closed late
9Dec06-7Crc	gd	1 1/16 Ⓣ	23 :482 1:123 1:423	ⒻCherokFrlc100k	76	2/8	85½	83¾	72	41½	1¾	Douglas R R	L116	*1.60	83-12	Rutherienne¾ Perfect Motion¾ Island Friend¾	Angled out, up late
12Nov06-4Crc	fm	1 1/16 Ⓣ	221 :471 1:122 1:431	ⒻMd Sp Wt 20k	74	4/10	76½	65¼	43	12½	16	Douglas R R	L118	*1.80	80-15	*Rutherienne*6 *Leap in the Sun*2¾ Classic Strike¾	Steadied start & turn

Daily Racing Form ***20160616. Santa Anita. 1 1/4 Miles. Turf. Thoroughbred***

Magical Fantasy

Own: Bienstock David, Mandabach, Paul and

Ch. f. 4 (Mar)
Sire: Diesis*GB (Sharpen Up*GB) $30,000
Dam: Kissing Gate (Easy Goer)
Br: Rodes S. Parrish & Charles Beach IV (Ky)
Tr: Gallagher Patrick(0 0 0 0 .00) 2009:(0 0 .00)

Life	17	6	4	0	$1,039,231	98	D.Fst	0	0	0	0	$0	-
2009	6	4	1	0	$764,800	98	Wet(280)	0	0	0	0	$0	-
							Synth	6	1	3	0	$66,746	98
2008	6	1	1	0	$265,685	92	Turf(334)	11	5	1	0	$972,485	98
Sa Ⓣ	2	2	0	0	$300,000	98	DstⓉ(332)	3	2	0	0	$300,000	98

10Oct09-40SA	fm	1¼Ⓣ	472 1:114 1:36 1:592 3↑	ⒻYlwRibbn-G1	98	1/8	66	65	53½	31½	1½	Solis A	LB123	*1.20	88-08	Magical Fantasy½ Visitno *Black Mamba*1½	4wd into str,held btwn
16Aug09-8Dmr	fm	1⅛Ⓣ	48 1:12 1:353 1:47 3↑	ⒻJCMabee-G1	98	3/9	74¾	74¾	74	53	11	Solis A	LB123	*2.20	88-12	*MagicalFantasy*1 *GottaHaveHer*½ Patricia'sGem½	4wd into lane,rallied
30May09-9Hol	fm	1⅛Ⓣ	483 1:121 1:36 1:48 +3↑	ⒻGamely-G1	98	5/9	73½	73½	63½	52¾	1nk	Solis A	LB123	6.10	81-18	*Magical Fantasy*nk Visitno Diamond Diva1¼	4wd into lane,rallied
18Apr09-9SA	fm	1¼Ⓣ	481 1:122 1:36 1:594 4↑	ⒻSntBrbrH-G2	97	1/8	41¼	43	53½	32½	1no	Solis A	LB117	3.00	86-12	*MagicalFantasy*no BlackMamba¾ ToquedeQued¾	Steadied 5/16,gamely
14Mar09-8SA	fst	1⅛◈	472 1:114 1:362 1:483 4↑	ⒻSMrgrtaH-G1	97	4/6	34	34½	32½	4¾	44½	Solis A	LB117	5.80	80-17	Life Is Sweet2½ Santa Teresita1¾ Modelnk	Btwn,3wd,willing late
15Feb09-8SA	fst	1⅛◈	50 1:141 1:374 1:493	ⒻLaCanada-G2	98	4/9	31½	32½	32½	21	2¾	Solis A	LB120	5.30	79-21	*Life Is Sweet*¾ MagicalFantasynk Bsharpsonatano	3wd into lane,gamely
30Nov08-7Hol	fm	1 Ⓣ	253 :49 1:12 1:352 3↑	ⒻMatriarc-G1	92	1/8	41½	41½	42	31½	42	Solis A	LB120	24.60	85-13	Cocoa Beach¾ Precious Kitten½ Visit¾	Pulled,bit tight 1/4
11Oct08-9Kee	fm	1⅛Ⓣ	47 1:113 1:354 1:48	ⒻQEIICup-G1	92	6/11	118¾	109	107¼	85	64½	Solis A	L121	8.90	94-06	Alwajeeha1¼ BcksetRhythmnk MyPrincessJess2	Rank, steadied, bobble
16Aug08-8Dmr	fm	1⅛Ⓣ	47 1:111 1:35 1:463	ⒻDMrOaks-G1	92	5/10	98¾	99¼	83¼	41½	12	Solis A	LB122	42.50	90-09	Magical Fantasy2 Bel Air Sizzle¾ Lethal Heatnk	Split foes,led,clear
5Jly08-9Hol	fm	1¼Ⓣ	47 1:104 1:35 2:002	ⒻAmrOksIn-G1	88	2/12	129¾	1210	96¾	85¼	65	Solis A	LB121	35.60	86-10	Pure Clan¾ Satan's Circus½ Clearly Foxy2¾	Pulled bit,3wd lane
7Jun08-7Hol	fm	1⅛Ⓣ	473 1:114 1:354 1:472 +	ⒻHnymoonH-G2	87	5/6	47	57½	43½	43	52½	Solis A	LB119	4.20	81-09	Misty Ocean¾ Bel Air Sizzle¾ Sweeter Still1	Saved ground to lane
10May08-7Hol	fm	1 Ⓣ	223 :461 1:104 1:353	ⒻSenorita-G3	86	5/8	611	78½	64	32½	2no	Solis A	LB117	13.40	86-14	Sweeter Stillno Magical Fantasy1¾ Bel AirSizzlenk	4wd into str,drift out

Previously trained by James Nicol

26Nov07 Lingfield (GB)	ft	1	◈ LH 1:391	Lingfield for Weddings Mdn Stks(polytrac	12	1hd	Callan N	124	*2.00	Magical Fantasyhd Agente Romano2 Valvigneres1	
Racing Post Rating:	67			Maiden 7900							*Rank in 3rd,2nd 2f over out,led over 1f out,just held*
10Nov07 Wolverhampton (GB)	ft	1 1/16	◈ LH 1:504	Maiden Auction Stks(polytrack)(1m,141y)	9	21	Egan J F	122	2.00	Mystery Star1 *Magical Fantasy*6 Tamasou2	
Racing Post Rating:	76			Maiden 9100							*Tracked in 3rd,led 2f out,headed over 1f out*
31Oct07 Kempton (GB)	ft	1	◈ RH 1:39	Kempton.co.uk Mdn Auction Stks(polytrack	13	22	Callan N	122	8.00	Sassy Gal2 Magical Fantasyno Moment's Notice2	
Racing Post Rating:	68			Maiden 6200							*Tracked leaders,brief bid over 1f out,saved 2nd*
11Sep07 Lingfield (GB)	ft	7f	◈ LH 1:251	ⒻEBF Maiden Stakes (polytrack)	11	41¼	Hughes R	126	7.00	Blue Rhapsody1 Red Iconno Riverscapehd	
Racing Post Rating:	72			Maiden 10900							*Led or dueled to 1f out,lost 2nd & 3rd near line*
11Aug07 Newmarket (GB)	fm	7f	Ⓣ Str 1:262	ⒻWyck Hall Stud Maiden Stakes	18	1111	Urbina O	126	66.00	Cape Amber3 Fifty1½ Redeemed1	
Racing Post Rating:	61			Maiden 14200							*Rated in mid-pack,drifted left 2f out,weakened*

Pure Clan

Own: Lakin Lewis G

Ch. f. 4 (Mar)
Sire: Pure Prize (Storm Cat) $12,500
Dam: Gather The Clan*Ire (General Assembly)
Br: A. Lakin & Sons, Inc. (Ky)
Tr: Holthus Robert E(0 0 0 0 .00) 2009:(0 0 .00)

Life	15	8	3	3	$1,627,498	98	D.Fst	4	2	1	1	$316,062	97
2009	4	2	1	1	$575,082	98	Wet(391)	1	0	0	1	$56,667	90
							Synth	0	0	0	0	$0	-
2008	7	2	2	2	$736,207	97	Turf(296)	10	6	2	1	$1,254,769	98
Sa Ⓣ	1	0	0	0	$0	91	DstⓉ(367)	5	3	0	1	$1,003,500	98

3Oct09-8Bel	sf	1¼Ⓣ	534 1:202 1:463 2:122 3↑	ⒻFlwrBIlv-G1	98	2/7	53	53	32½	21½	12¾	Leparoux J R	L121b	2.60	33-67	Pure Clan2¾ *Criticism*1¼ Queen of Hearts2¾	Split 4wide turn
8Aug09-8AP	gd	1 3/16Ⓣ	503 1:153 1:393 1:581 3↑	ⒻBeverlyD-G1	96	2/8	88	86¾	84¾	74¾	31½	Leparoux J R	L123b	*1.50	75-22	Dynaforce1¼ Alnadanank *Pure Clan*no	Best stride late 5wd
11Jly09-5AP	fm	1 3/16Ⓣ	494 1:133 1:374 1:551 3↑	ⒻModestyH-G3	96	1/5	54	44	53	1hd	12½	Leparoux J R	L122b	*.80	92-08	Pure Clan2½ Tizaqueenank *Dynaforce*1¼	4 wide move drew clear
6Jun09-10CD	fm	1 1/16Ⓣ	242 :49 1:134 1:43 3↑	ⒻMntJulpH-G3	95	1/6	64	63½	63½	42	2nk	Bridgmohan S X	L122b	2.50	88-13	Acomank *Pure Clan*4¾ Tizaqueena½	4 w, between, gaining
24Oct08-6OSA	fm	1¼Ⓣ	50 1:143 1:38 2:012 3↑	ⒻBCFMTrf-G1	91	10/10	108	109	1011	109¾	108½	Prado E S	LB118b	11.90	75-11	*Forever Together*¾ Sealy Hillhd ⒹWait a While¾	4wd hill,no rally

Placed 9th through disqualification

6Sep08-3Bel	yl	1⅛Ⓣ	494 1:143 1:392 1:514	ⒻGrdnCy-G1	94	5/8	57	57½	53½	62½	2½	Leparoux J R	L122b	*1.00e	65-34	Backseat Rhythm½ Pure Clannk Ariege1	Boxed in blocked 1/4pl
5Jly08-9Hol	fm	1¼Ⓣ	47 1:104 1:35 2:002	ⒻAmrOksIn-G1	96	1/12	96½	96¾	32	41½	1¾	Leparoux J R	LB121b	*2.50	91-10	Pure Clan¾ Satan's Circus½ Clearly Foxy2¾	Waited 1/8,split,game
14Jun08-7CD	fm	1⅛Ⓣ	492 1:14 1:38 1:494	ⒻRegret-G3	92	3/5	31½	31½	41¾	31½	12¾	Leparoux J R	L116b	*1.00	86-11	*Pure Clan*2¾ C J's Leelee1½ Zee Zee2½	In hand rail, driving
2May08-10CD	slyS	1⅛	484 1:124 1:371 1:50	ⒻKyOaks-G1	90	10/10	84¾	73½	63½	66½	35¾	Prado E S	L121b	4.00	80-15	Proud Spell5 Little Belle¾ *Pure Clan*hd	4 wide middle move
6Apr08-10OP	fst	1 1/16	241 :48 1:122 1:43	ⒻFantasy-G2	97	2/4	21½	21½	3½	33	31¼	Leparoux J R	L121b	2.00	96-13	Eight Belles¾ Alina½ Pure Clan11	Coming again late
16Mar08-9OP	fst	1 1/16	241 :483 1:131 1:434	ⒻHoneybee-G3	89	4/6	54½	53½	42	34½	21¼	Leparoux J R	L119b	2.00	92-09	*Eight Belles*1¼ Pure Clan2¼ Kadira8½	4w 1/4, willingly
24Nov07-9CD	fst	1 1/16	243 :484 1:13 1:432	ⒻGoldnRod-G2	83	1/8	62¾	52½	62½	31½	12	Leparoux J R	L119b	2.90	93-10	Pure Clan2 C J's Leelee¾ Turn Away1¾	Bobble,steadied,5w,drv
28Oct07-10CD	fst	1	222 :454 1:12 1:381	ⒻPocahnts-G3	80	9/14	129½	126½	114½	54	11½	Leparoux J R	L119b	10.30	78-20	*Pure Clan*1½ Authenicat1 Sky Mom½	Bobble start,squeezed
10Oct07-5Kee	fm	1 Ⓣ	243 :492 1:143 1:382	ⒻAlw 50590N2L	74	6/9	52½	63¾	74½	5¾	11¾	Leparoux J R	L115b	2.50	75-20	*Pure Clan*1¾ Through the Clouds1½ VictorySting½	6w,between lane,drvg
26Aug07-11ElP	fm	5½f Ⓣ	221 :463 :58 1:04	ⒻMd Sp Wt 18k	69	6/8	8	23½	22	15	17¾	Mojica O	L120b	*1.50	84-16	*PureCln*7¾ AbsolutelyCindy4 AncientProphecy1½	Much best,ridden out

Midday (GB)

Own: Juddmonte Farms Inc

B. f. 3 (Mar)
Sire: Oasis Dream*GB (Green Desert)
Dam: Midsummer*GB (Kingmambo)
Br: Juddmonte Farms Ltd (GB)
Tr: Cecil Henry(0 0 0 0 .00) 2009:(0 0 .00)

Life	10	3	2	3	$481,105	-	D.Fst	0	0	0	0	$0	-
2009	6	2	2	2	$465,407	-	Wet(251*)	0	0	0	0	$0	-
							Synth	0	0	0	0	$0	-
2008	4	1	0	1	$15,698	-	Turf(364)	10	3	2	3	$481,105	-
Sa Ⓣ	0	0	0	0	$0	-	DstⓉ(310)	3	1	1	1	$236,781	-

4Oct09 Longchamp (Fr)	gd	*1¼ Ⓣ	RH 2:014 3↑	ⒻPrix de l'Opera-G1	9	31½	Queally T P	123	3.80	Shalanaya1½ Board Meetingno *Midday*¾	
Racing Post Rating:	111			Stk 364000							*Trckd in 4th,led over 1f to 100y out,lost 2nd late.AlpineRose4th*
1Aug09 Goodwood (GB)	sf	1¼ Ⓣ	RH 2:092 3↑	ⒻNassau Stakes-G1	10	12¼	Queally T P	122	5.50	Midday2¼ *Rainbow View*½ Moneycantbuymelove2¼	
Racing Post Rating:	121			Stk 334000							*Tracked in 4th,led 2f out,drew clear 1f out*
12Jly09 Curragh (Ire)	hy	1½ Ⓣ	RH 2:454	ⒻIrish Oaks-G1	10	37½	Queally T P	126	4.50	Sariska3 Roses For The Lady4½ *Midday*4	
Racing Post Rating:	105			Stk 697500							*Trckd in 3rd,2nd 3f out,lost 2nd over 1f out.RomanEmpress6th*
5Jun09 Epsom (GB)	gd	1½ Ⓣ	LH 2:351	ⒻEnglish Oaks-G1	10	2hd	Queally T P	126	5.00	*Sariska*hd Midday2½ High Heeled4½	
Racing Post Rating:	121			Stk 566500							*Rated in 6th,carried left 3f out,3rd 2f out,gamely.RainbowView4th*
9May09 Lingfield (GB)	gf	1 7/16 Ⓣ	LH 2:302	ⒻLingfield Oaks Trial (Listed)	9	16	Queally T P	124	*2.50	Midday6 July Jasmine¾ Tottienk	
Racing Post Rating:	106			Stk 76200							*Tracked in 4th,led over 2f out,quickly clear*
22Apr09 Epsom (GB)	gd	1¼ Ⓣ	LH 2:084	Blue Riband Trial Stakes	7	21¼	Queally T P	122	3.30	Debussy1¼ *Midday*¾ Popmurphy7	
Racing Post Rating:	97			Alw 29400							*Tracked in 3rd,rail bid to lead 2-1/2f out,headed over 1f out*
1Nov08 Newmarket (GB)	gs	1	Ⓣ Str 1:402	ⒻEBF Montrose Stakes (Listed)	13	41¼	Mullen R	124	9.00	Enticementno Super Sleuth¾ Splashdown½	
Racing Post Rating:	96			Stk 48300							*Rated towards rear,finished well*
19Sep08 Newmarket (GB)	gf	1	Ⓣ Str 1:374	ⒻEBF Oriental Foods Maiden Stakes	18	1no	Durcan T E	126	*.90	Middayno Three Moons3 Featherweighthd	
Racing Post Rating:	84			Maiden 18200							*Rated in 6th,bid 2f out,dueled 1f out,gamely prevailed*
22Aug08 Newmarket (GB)	gd	7f	Ⓣ Str 1:24	ⒻEBF Maiden Stakes	17	31	Durcan T E	126	*1.35	Golden Stream1 Uvinzano *Midday*2¾	
Racing Post Rating:	86			Maiden 14100							*Mid-pack,drifted right halfway,outfinished*
31Jly08 Goodwood (GB)	gf	7f	Ⓣ RH 1:273	ⒻEBF New Ham Maiden Stakes	15	77¾	Durcan T E	126	10.00	Pachattack1¼ Careless Whisper2¾ Persian Memories1	
Racing Post Rating:	62			Maiden 39600							*Broke in tangle,rated in 14th,some late progress*

Daily Racing Form — *20160616. Santa Anita. 1 1/4 Miles. Turf. Thoroughbred*

Dynaforce
Own: Chandler Dr. John A

B. m. 6 (Mar)
Sire: Dynaformer (Roberto) $150,000
Dam: Aletta Maria (Diesis*GB)
Br: Dr. John A. Chandler (Ky)
Tr: Mott William I(0 0 0 0 .00) 2009:(0 0 .00)

Life	16	5	3	3	$1,086,772	104	D.Fst	0	0	0	0	$0	–
2009	4	1	0	1	$472,000	97	Wet(296)	0	0	0	0	$0	–
							Synth	0	0	0	0	$0	–
2008	5	1	2	0	$513,267	104	Turf(345)	16	5	3	3	$1,086,772	104
Sa ⓣ	1	0	0	0	$0	98	Dstⓣ(353)	10	3	2	2	$939,889	104

3Oct09-8Bel	sf	1¼ [T]	53^4 $1{:}20^2$ $1{:}46^3$ $2{:}12^2$	3↑ⒻFlwrBlIv-G1	**61**	3/7	3^1	$3^{1\frac{1}{2}}$	5^4	6^{11}	$6^{20\frac{3}{4}}$	Desormeaux K J	L123	*2.30	12-67	Pure Clan$^{2\frac{3}{4}}$ *Criticism*$^{1\frac{1}{4}}$ Queen of Hearts$^{2\frac{3}{4}}$	Rail trip tired
8Aug09-8AP	gd	1 3/16 ⓣ	50^3 $1{:}15^3$ $1{:}39^3$ $1{:}58^1$	3↑ⒻBeverlyD-G1	**97**	7/8	$2^{1\frac{1}{2}}$	2^2	2^1	2^{hd}	$1^{1\frac{1}{4}}$	Desormeaux K J	L123	7.60	77-22	Dynaforce$^{1\frac{1}{4}}$ Alnadana^{nk} *Pure Clan*^{no}	Stalked, drew clear
11Jly09-5AP	fm	1 1/16 ⓣ	49^4 $1{:}13^3$ $1{:}37^4$ $1{:}55^1$	3↑ⒻModestyH-G3	**92**	5/5	2^{hd}	$2^{\frac{1}{2}}$	$2^{1\frac{1}{2}}$	3^1	$3^{2\frac{3}{4}}$	Albarado R J	L120	2.30	89-08	Pure Clan$^{2\frac{1}{2}}$ Tizaqueena^{nk} *Dynaforce*$^{1\frac{1}{4}}$	Bid lane, outfinished
16May09-7Pim	fm	1 1/16 ⓣ	23^4 $:48^2$ $1{:}12^1$ $1{:}41^4$	3↑ⒻGalrettH-G3	**85**	7/7	$2^{\frac{1}{2}}$	$2^{\frac{1}{2}}$	2^{hd}	3^1	$5^{4\frac{1}{4}}$	Gomez G K	L122	*.90	88-11	Social Queen^{hd} *All Is Vanity*$^{2\frac{1}{4}}$ Tejida^1	Pressed pace, gave way
24Oct08-6OSA	fm	1¼ ⓣ	50 $1{:}14^3$ 1:38 $2{:}01^2$	3↑ⒻBCFMTrf-G1	**98**	6/10	$5^{3\frac{1}{2}}$	$6^{3\frac{1}{2}}$	$8^{5\frac{1}{4}}$	$9^{4\frac{3}{4}}$	8^4	Garcia Alan	LB123	14.20	80-11	*Forever Together*$^{\frac{3}{4}}$ Sealy Hill^{hd} [D]Wait a While$^{\frac{3}{4}}$	Inside,steadied 1/8
Placed 7th through disqualification																	
27Sep08-7Bel	yl	1¼ [T]	52^4 $1{:}19^1$ $1{:}43^2$ $2{:}07^2$	3↑ⒻFlwrBlIv-G1	**104**	3/5	$1^{1\frac{1}{2}}$	1^1	1^{hd}	1^2	1^4	Garcia Alan	L119	3.30	58-42	Dynaforce^4 Mauralakana^{nk} Communique$^{5\frac{1}{2}}$	Roused from 3/8's
1Sep08-8Sar	fm	1⅜ [T]	47^2 $1{:}11^3$ $1{:}35^4$ $2{:}11^3$	3↑ⒻGlenFlsH-G3	**86**	3/6	$3^{1\frac{1}{2}}$	2^1	2^2	5^4	$5^{7\frac{1}{2}}$	Desormeaux K J	L118	*.55	99-04	Hostess^{nk} Palmilla$^{2\frac{3}{4}}$ Jade Queen$^{3\frac{1}{2}}$	Steadied early, tired
26Jly08-7Sar	gd	1⅛ ⓣ	46^4 $1{:}10^4$ $1{:}34^3$ $1{:}46^2$	3↑ⒻDiana-G1	**104**	2/10	$2^{1\frac{1}{2}}$	$2^{5\frac{1}{2}}$	2^3	$1^{\frac{1}{2}}$	$2^{\frac{3}{4}}$	Desormeaux K J	L118	3.40	93-06	Forever Together$^{\frac{3}{4}}$ Dynaforce$^{3\frac{1}{2}}$ Rutherienne^{no}	Yielded late
21Jun08-9Bel	fm	1¼ [T]	49^3 $1{:}13^4$ 1:38 $2{:}01^1$	3↑ⒻNewYork-G2	**101**	1/5	$2^{1\frac{1}{2}}$	2^1	2^1	$3^{\frac{1}{2}}$	2^{nk}	Velazquez J R	L116	2.80	89-14	*Mauralakana*^{nk} Dynaforce^{nk} *Hostess*$^{1\frac{1}{4}}$	Rated wide, game

Previously trained by Andre Fabre

19Aug07 Deauville (Fr)	sf	*1¼ ⓣ	RH 2:11	4↑ ⒻPrix Jean Romanet-G2	Stk 175000	11	3^2	Pasquier S	123	7.00	*Satwa Queen*^{no} Bahia Breeze^2 Dynaforce^{nk}	*Trckd in 3rd,brief bid,outfinished,GreenGirl5th,HeavenSent6th*
Racing Post Rating: 105												
17Jly07 Vichy (Fr)	sf	*1½ ⓣ	RH 2:35	4↑ Prix de Clermont-Ferrand	Alw 39900	7	$1^{1\frac{1}{2}}$	Pasquier S	120	*1.80	Dynaforce$^{1\frac{1}{2}}$ Naukos^{nk} Penkinella$^{1\frac{1}{2}}$	*Tracked leader,led 2-1/2f out,held well*
24Oct06 Saint-Cloud (Fr)	sf	*1 5/16 ⓣ	LH $2{:}19^3$	3↑ ⒻPrix de Flore-G3	Stk 100500	7	$5^{3\frac{3}{4}}$	Soumillon C	120	*1.40	Miss Salvador^{no} Wingspan^3 Bastet$^{\frac{1}{2}}$	*Trckd leader,3rd 3f out,drifted right,last 1-1/2f out,up for 5th*
Racing Post Rating: 102												
29Sep06 Chantilly (Fr)	gs	*1¼ ⓣ	RH $2{:}07^2$	ⒻPrix Charles Laffitte (Listed)	Stk 63500	11	1^{nk}	Pasquier S	123	4.10	Dynaforce^{nk} *Sanaya*$^{1\frac{1}{2}}$ Rose Melody$^{\frac{1}{2}}$	*Tracked leaders,lacked room 2f out,led near line*
Racing Post Rating: 103												
3Sep06 Longchamp (Fr)	gs	*1⅛ ⓣ	RH $1{:}56^1$	ⒻPrix de Liancourt (1 1/8m,55y) (Listed)	Stk 64200	11	$3^{2\frac{1}{2}}$	Fallon K	123	15.00	Lahudood$^{2\frac{1}{2}}$ Heaven's Cause^{no} *Dynaforce*^{no}	*Wide in 6th,2nd over 1f out,lost duel for 2nd*
Racing Post Rating: 98												
13May06 Lion dAngers (Fr)	gd	*1¼ ⓣ	LH $2{:}14^3$	ⒻPrix Christian de Tredern	Alw 28400	9	$2^{2\frac{1}{2}}$	Sautjeau M	128	1.80	Flow Chart$^{2\frac{1}{2}}$ Dynaforce^1 Isobel Baillie^{no}	*Led to 100y out,second best*
7Apr06 La Teste Buch (Fr)	sf	*1 ⓣ	RH $1{:}39^3$	Prix des Roses	Alw 22000	10	$1^{1\frac{1}{2}}$	Sautjeau M	119	8.50	Dynaforce$^{1\frac{1}{2}}$ Scamper^2 Keladora$^{\frac{3}{4}}$	*Tracked leader,led over 1f out,driving*

Maram
Own: Woods Karen N. and Khaled, Saud bin

Dk. b or b. f. 3 (Feb)
Sire: Sahm (Mr. Prospector) $5,000
Dam: American Dreamer (Quest for Fame*GB)
Br: Palides Investments N. V., Inc. & Hair 'Em Corporation (Ky)
Tr: Brown Chad C(0 0 0 0 .00) 2009:(0 0 .00)

Life	5	4	0	1	$799,520	92	D.Fst	0	0	0	0	$0	–
2009	2	1	0	1	$55,400	92	Wet(342)	0	0	0	0	$0	–
							Synth	0	0	0	0	$0	–
2008	3	3	0	0	$744,120	87	Turf(335)	5	4	0	1	$799,520	92
Sa ⓣ	1	1	0	0	$621,000	87	Dstⓣ(314)	0	0	0	0	$0	–

12Oct09-8Bel	fm	1 ⓣ	23^1 $:47^1$ $1{:}10^4$ 1:34	ⒻPebbles110k	**92**	1/9	$8^{4\frac{3}{4}}$	$8^{3\frac{3}{4}}$	$8^{4\frac{3}{4}}$	$6^{2\frac{3}{4}}$	3^{nk}	Lezcano J	L121	*1.45	90-15	Miss Catalyst^{nk} Pull Dancer^{no} Maram^1	Broke slow 5wide
8Aug09-8Sar	fm	1 [T]	23^2 :47 $1{:}10^2$ $1{:}34^3$	ⒻJHettinger74k	**90**	5/8	$5^{3\frac{1}{2}}$	5^3	$3^{1\frac{1}{2}}$	1^{hd}	$1^{\frac{1}{2}}$	Lezcano J	L118	*2.50	97-06	Maram$^{\frac{1}{2}}$ Bluegrass Princess^{nk} Kiawah Cat$^{1\frac{1}{4}}$	3wide, prevailed
24Oct08-4OSA	fm	1 ⓣ	22^2 $:45^4$ 1:10 1:35	ⒻBCJuvFlTrf1053k	**87**	3/12	$7^{4\frac{3}{4}}$	$7^{8\frac{1}{4}}$	5^5	$2^{2\frac{1}{2}}$	1no	Lezcano J	LB122	11.10	89-11	*Maram*^{no} Heart Shaped^1 *Laragh*^{1}	3wd into lane,rallied
1Oct08-7Bel	yl	1 1/16 ⓣ	24^4 $:49^2$ $1{:}14^3$ 1:46	ⒻMsGrillo-G3	**81**	7/11	$4^{2\frac{1}{2}}$	6^3	4^2	3^1	1^{nk}	Lezcano J	L117	6.60	66-34	*Maram*^{nk} Freedom Rings^{hd} *My Magic Moment*^{nk}	4w, up final strides
25Aug08-5Sar	fm	1 1/16 ⓣ	23^1 $:47^2$ $1{:}12^2$ $1{:}42^2$	ⒻMd 75000	**70**	5/9	5^3	6^5	6^6	2^{hd}	$1^{1\frac{1}{2}}$	Leparoux J R	L120	7.50	88-09	*Maram*$^{1\frac{1}{2}}$ Outstanding Henny^{nk} Lovamor$^{3\frac{1}{4}}$	4wide move, drew clear

SIXTH RACE

Oak Tree at SA

NOVEMBER 6, 2009

1¼ MILES. (Turf) (1.57) 11TH RUNNING OF THE EMIRATES AIRLINE BREEDERS' CUP FILLY AND MARE TURF. Grade I. Purse $2,000,000 FOR FILLIES AND MARES, THREE YEAR OLDS AND UPWARD. Northern Hemisphere Three-Year-Olds, 120 lbs.; Older, 124 lbs. Southern Hemisphere Three-Year-Olds, 115 lbs. Older, 124 lbs. $20,000 to pre-enter, $40,000 to enter, with guaranteed $2 million purse including nominator awards of which 54% to the owner of the winner, 18% to second, 9.9% to third, 6% to fourth and 3% to fifth; plus stallion nominator awards of 3% to the winner, 1% to second and 0.55% to third and foal nominator awards of 3% to the winner,1% to second and 0.55% to third.

Value of Race: $1,818,000 Winner $1,080,000; second $360,000; third $198,000; fourth $120,000; fifth $60,000. Mutuel Pool $2,309,041.00 Exacta Pool $1,351,496.00 Trifecta Pool $960,745.00 Superfecta Pool $423,026.00

Last Raced	Horse	M/Eqt.	A.	Wt	PP	¼	½	¾	1	Str	Fin	Jockey	Odds $1
40ct09 LCH^{3}	Midday-GB	LB	3	120	6	$5^{2\frac{1}{2}}$	5^{1}	3^{1}	$3^{\frac{1}{2}}$	2^{2}	1^{1}	Queally T P	2.30
30ct09 ^{8}Bel^{1}	Pure Clan	LB b	4	124	5	$7^{\frac{1}{2}}$	$7^{\frac{1}{2}}$	7^{2}	7^{1}	$6^{\frac{1}{2}}$	$2^{1\frac{1}{4}}$	Gomez G K	7.60
100ct09 ^{7}Kee^{3}	Forever Together	LB	5	124	2	8	8	8	8	8	3^{nk}	Leparoux J R	2.20
100ct09 ^{4}OSA^{2}	Visit-GB	LB	4	124	1	1^{1}	$1^{\frac{1}{2}}$	$1^{1\frac{1}{2}}$	1^{2}	$1^{\frac{1}{2}}$	4no	Velazquez J R	11.30
100ct09 ^{4}OSA^{1}	Magical Fantasy	LB	4	124	4	6^{1}	$6^{1\frac{1}{2}}$	$6^{1\frac{1}{2}}$	$6^{2\frac{1}{2}}$	$4^{\frac{1}{2}}$	5^{1}	Solis A	4.50
120ct09 ^{8}Bel^{3}	Maram	LB	3	120	8	4^{1}	4^{hd}	5^{1}	5^{hd}	5^{hd}	$6^{\frac{1}{2}}$	Lezcano J	16.10
19Sep09 ^{4}Bel^{1}	Rutherienne	LB	5	124	3	$3^{\frac{1}{2}}$	3^{1}	$4^{1\frac{1}{2}}$	$4^{1\frac{1}{2}}$	$3^{1\frac{1}{2}}$	$7^{4\frac{1}{4}}$	Garcia Alan	13.00
30ct09 ^{8}Bel^{6}	Dynaforce	LB	6	124	7	2^{1}	$2^{1\frac{1}{2}}$	$2^{\frac{1}{2}}$	2^{hd}	7^{1}	8	Desormeaux K J	13.50

OFF AT 2:25 Start Good. Won driving. Course firm.

TIME :24, :48^{4}, 1:12^{4}, 1:36, 1:59 (:24.14, :48.83, 1:12.95, 1:36.08, 1:59.14)

$2 Mutuel Prices:				
	6 -MIDDAY-GB	6.60	4.80	3.00
	5 -PURE CLAN		7.80	4.00
	2 -FOREVER TOGETHER			2.40

$1 EXACTA 6-5 PAID $26.80 $1 TRIFECTA 6-5-2 PAID $95.00 $1 SUPERFECTA 6-5-2-1 PAID $536.50

B. f, (Mar), by Oasis Dream-GB - Midsummer-GB, by Kingmambo. Trainer Cecil Henry. Bred by Juddmonte Farms Ltd (GB).

MIDDAY (GB) pulled a bit while being angled to the inside on the hill, stalked inside, moved up along the fence on the backstretch, continued inside on the second turn, bid along the rail in the stretch, gained the lead past the eighth pole, kicked clear under urging and held gamely. PURE CLAN allowed to settle outside a rival then just off the rail, came out some into the stretch, split rivals in midstretch then rallied along the inside for the place. FOREVER TOGETHER in a bit tight on the hill, chased inside, came out some on the second turn and into the stretch and just got the show outside foes on the line. VISIT (GB) pulled her way to the early lead inside, dueled on the first turn, inched away again on the backstretch and second turn, came out some into the stretch, battled outside the winner in midstretch, could not match either of the top pair in the final furlong and just lost third. MAGICAL FANTASY settled just off the rail then outside a rival, came out leaving the second turn and four wide into the stretch and just missed a minor award between horses late. MARAM four wide on the hill, angled in and stalked outside a rival then a bit off the fence, came out three deep into the stretch, was between horses in the drive and could not summon the necessary late kick. RUTHERIENNE pulled her way between horses then stalked just off the rail, went three deep leaving the second turn and into the stretch and lacked the needed response. DYNAFORCE three deep early, prompted the pace outside VISIT then stalked just off the rail, was between horses leaving the second turn and weakened.

Owners- 1, Juddmonte Farms Inc; 2, Lakin Lewis G; 3, Augustin Stable; 4, Juddmonte Farms Inc; 5, Bienstock&Mandabach&Winner; 6, Woods Karen N and Khaled Saud bin; 7, Virginia Kraft Payson LLC; 8, Chandler Dr John A

Trainers- 1, Cecil Henry; 2, Holthus Robert E; 3, Sheppard Jonathan E; 4, Frankel Robert; 5, Gallagher Patrick; 6, Brown Chad C; 7, Clement Christophe; 8, Mott William I

$2 Daily Double (8-6) Paid $93.00 ; Daily Double Pool $170,036 .

$1 Pick Three (10-8-6) Paid $423.60 ; Pick Three Pool $585,519 .

The handicapping by the author before the race was as follows. Midday was racing regularly so there was no problem with injuries and she was steadily building up to this race. She was racing with older fillies in four consecutive Grade 1 races so she is used to stiff competition and has finished in the money in all these races, especially at the Nassau Stakes where she beat a formidable Rainbow View and came in first. She also beat Rainbow View in a previous Grade 1 race and came in second. In her last 10 races, she finished in the money eight times. Her life record is 10 wins, 3 places and 2 shows exclusively on the soft turf in Europe where it rains with some regularity so she might even do better on firm footing on the firm turf at Santa Anita Park where it doesn't rain often. There are no speed figures for her but we know she has done well in her last six races so her speed figures are probably pretty high and are rising, maybe even peaking for this race. Her threats are Forever Together who has impressive speed figures but who has not raced against strong competition, Visit who has not been winning as of late, Pure Clan who had a miserable 10th place finish not long ago but is coming on however against weak competition, and Magical Fantasy who has won her last four last races but against weak competition.

Chapter 6

BETTING STRATEGIES

Of course you will consider a win bet on your horse and you can also bet your horse to place (in second place) or to show (in third place), or to win, place and show "across the board". If you wager only to place, your horse must finish first or second for you to get the place payoff. If you wager only to show, your horse must finish first, second, or third for you to get the show payoff.

At the racetrack, you will see the odds of winning for every horse in a race on the toteboard, a large electronic display placed in the infield facing the stands, and on TV screens at many locations inside the track. Odds are also televised. Before the race, the toteboard will also show for each horse, the dollar amount wagered on win, place and show bets, and the total wagering pools of the win, place and show bets in the race. For a two dollar exacta of a horse on top of every horse in the race, it will show the prospective payoffs. For a two dollar double of a horse with every horse in the next race, it will show the prospective payoffs.

In the examples below, a 3/5 shot is expressed as 3 to 5, and 7 is expressed as 7 to 1. As displayed on the toteboard, the odds before the race of every horse to win, and after the race the payoffs for the win, place and show $2.00 bets are as follows:

Odds Before The Race	*Displayed Payoffs For the Odds After The Race*
1/9 (extreme favorite)	1/9 will arbitrarily be displayed for odds from 1/9 and lower before the race. Depending on the actual odds at the start of the race, the high payoff resulting from 1/9 will be $2.20

	($2.00 plus $.20 equals $2.20 so there will be a $.20 payoff for a $2.00 bet and a $.10 payoff for a $1.00 bet). For odds lower than 1/9, the lowest payoff will be $2.10 ($2.00 plus $.10 equals $2.10 so there will be a $.10 payoff for a $2.00 bet and a $.05 payoff for a $1.00 bet).
1/5	$2.40 ($2.00 plus forty cents equals $2.40 so there will be a $ .40 payoff for a $2.00 bet and a $ .20 payoff for a $1.00 bet).
2/5	$2.80 ($2.00 plus eighty cents equals $2.80 so there will be an $ .80 payoff for a $2.00 bet and a $ .40 payoff for a $1.00 bet).
1/2	$3.00 ($2.00 plus $1.00 equals $3.00 so there will be a $1.00 payoff for a $2.00 bet and a $, 50 payoff for a $1.00 bet).
3/5	$3.20 ($2.00 plus $1.20 equals $3.20 so there will be a $1.20 payoff for a $2.00 bet and a $ .60 payoff for a $1.00 bet).
4/5	$3.60 ($2.00 plus $1.60 equals $3.60 so there will be an $1.60 payoff for a $2.00 bet and an $ .80 payoff for a $1.00 bet).
1 (even odds)	$4.00 ($2.00 plus $2.00 equals $4.00 so there will be a $2.00 payoff for a $2.00 bet and a $1.00 payoff for a $1.00 bet).
6/5	$4.40 ($2.00 plus $2.40 equals $4.40 so there will be a $2.40 payoff for a $2.00 bet and a $1.20 payoff for a $1.00 bet).
7/5	$4.80 ($2.00 plus $2.80 equals $4.80 so there will be a $2.80 payoff for a $2.00 bet and a $1.40 payoff for a $1.00 bet).
3/2	$5.00 ($2.00 plus $3.00 equals $5.00 so there will be a $3.00 payoff for a $2.00 bet and a $1.50 payoff for a $1.00 bet).
8/5	$5.20 ($2.00 plus $3.20 equals $5.20 so there will be a $3.20 payoff for a $2.00 bet and a $1.60 payoff for a $1.00 bet).
9/5	$5.60 ($2.00 plus $3.60 equals $5.60 so there will be a $3.60 payoff for a $2.00 bet and a $1.80 payoff for a $1.00 bet).

2	\$6.00 (\$2.00 plus \$4.00 equals \$6.00 so there will be a \$4.00 payoff for a \$2.00 bet and a \$2.00 payoff for a \$1.00 bet).
5/2	\$7.00 (\$2.00 plus \$5.00 equals \$7.00 so there will be a \$5.00 payoff for a \$2.00 bet and a \$2.50 payoff for a \$1.00 bet).
3	\$8.00 (\$2.00 plus \$6.00 equals \$8.00 so there will be a \$6.00 payoff for a \$2.00 bet and a \$3.00 payoff for a \$1.00 bet).
7/2	\$9.00 (\$2.00 plus \$7.00 equals \$9.00 so there will be a \$7.00 payoff for a \$2.00 bet and a \$3.50 payoff for a \$1.00 bet).
4	\$10.00 (\$2.00 plus \$8.00 equals \$10.00 so there will be an \$8.00 payoff for a \$2.00 bet and a \$4.00 payoff for a \$1.00 bet).
9/2	\$11.00 (\$2.00 plus \$9.00 equals \$11.00 so there will be a \$9.00 payoff for a \$2.00 bet and a \$4.50 payoff for a \$1.00 bet).
5	\$12.00 (\$2.00 plus \$10.00 equals \$12.00 so there will be a \$10.00 payoff for a \$2.00 bet and a \$5.00 payoff for a \$1.00 bet).
6	\$14.00 (\$2.00 plus \$12.00 equals \$14.00 so there will be a \$12.00 payoff for a \$2.00 bet and a \$6.00 payoff for a \$1.00 bet).
7	\$16.00 (\$2.00 plus \$14.00 equals \$16.00 so there will be a \$14.00 payoff for a \$2.00 bet and a \$7.00 payoff for a \$1.00 bet).
8	\$18.00 (\$2.00 plus \$16.00 equals \$18.00 so there will be a \$16.00 payoff for a \$2.00 bet and an \$8.00 payoff for a \$1.00 bet).
9	\$20.00 (\$2.00 plus \$18.00 equals \$20.00 so there will be an \$18.00 payoff for a \$2.00 bet and a \$9.00 payoff for a \$1.00 bet).

10 $22.00 ($2.00 plus $20.00 equals $22.00 so there will be a $20.00 payoff for a $2.00 bet and a $10.00 payoff for a $1.00 bet).

11 $24.00 ($2.00 plus $22.00 equals $24.00 so there will be a $22.00 payoff for a $2.00 bet and an $11.00 payoff for a $1.00 bet).

12 $26.00 ($2.00 plus $24.00 equals $26.00 so there will be a $24.00 payoff for a $2.00 bet and a $12.00 payoff for a $1.00 bet).

13 $28.00 ($2.00 plus $26.00 equals $28.00 so there will be a $26.00 payoff for a $2.00 bet and a $13.00 payoff for a $1.00 bet).

14 $30.00 ($2.00 plus $28.00 equals $30.00 so there will be a $28.00 payoff for a $2.00 bet and a $14.00 payoff for a $1.00 bet).

15 $32.00 ($2.00 plus $30.00 equals $32.00 so there will be a $30.00 payoff for a $2.00 bet and a $15.00 payoff for a $1.00 bet).

16 $34.00 ($2.00 plus $32.00 equals $34.00 so there will be a $32.00 payoff for a $2.00 bet and a $16.00 payoff for a $1.00 bet).

17 $36.00 ($2.00 plus $34.00 equals $36.00 so there will be a $34.00 payoff for a $2.00 bet and a $17.00 payoff for a $1.00 bet).

18 $38.00 ($2.00 plus $36.00 equals $38.00 so there will be a $36.00 payoff for a $2.00 bet and an $18.00 payoff for a $1.00 bet).

19 $40.00 ($2.00 plus $38.00 equals $40.00 so there will be a $38.00 payoff for a $2.00 bet and a $19.00 payoff for a $1.00 bet).

20 $42.00 ($2.00 plus $40.00 equals $42.00 so there will be a $40.00 payoff for a $2.00 bet and a $20.00 payoff for a $1.00 bet).

21 $44.00 ($2.00 plus $42.00 equals $44.00 so there will be a $42.00 payoff for a $2.00 bet and a $21.00 payoff for a $1.00 bet).

22 $46.00 ($2.00 plus $44.00 equals $46.00 so there will be a $44.00 payoff for a $2.00 bet and a $22.00 payoff for a $1.00 bet).

23 $48.00 ($2.00 plus $46.00 equals $48.00 so there will be a $46.00 payoff for a $2.00 bet and a $23.00 payoff for a $1.00 bet).

24 $50.00 ($2.00 plus $48.00 equals $50.00 so there will be a $48.00 payoff for a $2.00 bet and a $24.00 payoff for a $1.00 bet).

25 $52.00 ($2.00 plus $50.00 equals $52.00 so there will be a $50.00 payoff for a $2.00 bet and a $25.00 payoff for a $1.00 bet).

26 $54.00 ($2.00 plus $52.00 equals $54.00 so there will be a $52.00 payoff for a $2.00 bet and a $26.00 payoff for a $1.00 bet).

27 $56.00 ($2.00 plus $54.00 equals $56.00 so there will be a $54.00 payoff for a $2.00 bet and a $27.00 payoff for a $1.00 bet).

28 $58.00 ($2.00 plus $56.00 equals $58.00 so there will be a $56.00 payoff for a $2.00 bet and a $28.00 payoff for a $1.00 bet).

29 $60.00 ($2.00 plus $58.00 equals $60.00 so there will be a $58.00 payoff for a $2.00 bet and a $29.00 payoff for a $1.00 bet).

30 (long shot)	$62.00 ($2.00 plus $60.00 equals $62.00 so there will be a $60.00 payoff for a $2.00 bet and a $30.00 payoff for a $1.00 bet).
and so on	and so on

To see your approximate payoff with any of the above odds, simply multiply the amount you wagered by the payoff for a 1.00 bet. Realize that your actual payoff might be a bit different, for example on a 10 to 1 shot, the amount that was bet on your 10 to 1 horse could result in odds that are not exactly 10 to 1 so you could get more or less than $10.00 for a $1.00 bet. Also realize that the 10 to 1 odds can change all the way up until post time depending on how much money was wagered on the horse. Your payoff will also depend on the takeout of the track and the type of bet. A track's takeout can be fifteen percent for a regular win, place or show bet and up to twenty-five percent of an exotic bet like the Pick 6.

In a race, you can place various bets (wagers) of various minimum amounts depending on the racetrack and the race. There are also slightly different types of bets in different countries. You can usually bet an exacta with your horse on top to win and another horse under it to arrive in second place. You can bet an exacta box with your horse on top and underneath another horse. You might want to bet an exacta "wheel" putting your horse on top of every horse in the race (maybe leaving out the favorites for a good payoff in a par or partial wheel). For insurance, you might also want to play an exacta "wheel" with every horse in the race on top of your horse (maybe leaving out the favorites for a good payoff in a par or partial wheel). You can also play a graduated wheel where you play for example one, two and three dollar exactas in the same wheel.

You can put more than two horses in a single exacta, boxing 3 or 4 horses or more in a single exacta box bet. Realize that if you bet "chalk" exactas which means you are including favorites in the exacta, your bet might cost you more than the payoff. There are 50 cent exactas if you want to experiment. You can also play your horse in a $2.00 triple, calling the first three horses to finish in the race, or you can box your horse with two other horses in every combination in the triple for twelve dollars.

You can bet a horse to win a race together with another horse to win the following race. This is known as a double. There might be several doubles allowed in a card for a day. You must place a double bet before the start of the first race in the double. You might want to bet a "forward wheel" putting your horse with every horse in the next race (maybe leaving out the favorites for a good payoff in a par or partial wheel). For insurance, you might also want to play a "backward wheel" with every horse in the next race with your horse (maybe leaving out the favorites for a good payoff in a par or partial wheel). If you are alive in the second part of a double, you can bet exactas in that race to really pound the horse you picked in it to win.

You can play a "Pick 6" which means you have to pick six winners in six consecutive races. You must place this bet before the first race in the Pick 6. There is a twenty cent "Rainbow Pick 6" at Gulfstream Park in Florida. Twenty cents have been known to win $18,000 when there is a huge carryover (when nobody has hit the Rainbow Pick 6 for more than a few days).

You can also play a "Pick 3" or "Pick 4" in a card but the bet must be placed before the first race in the Pick 3 or Pick 4.

Do not bet a horse that says "Entered for Main Track Only" in the DRF. You have enough to figure out!

Very important - when you are calling in your bet, you must give the track program number of the horse in the favorable post position, NOT the post position of the horse.

Chapter 7

ARE YOU LUCKY ON THE DAY OF THE RACE?

Is it a good day for you personally to wager on a race? Although you might think your luck has nothing to do with picking a winner using the analytic, objective tools described above, I'm afraid that that is just not the case. The astrological influences in your life at the time of the race will very much decide whether you have the best chance to win. Instead of spending considerable time and effort trying to determine your lucky days (looking at Jupiter transits to your natal planets, solar return planets, lunar return planets, etc.) visit the following website that has lucky day software that does all of this for you:

http://www.luckydays.tv/index.html
http://www.luckydays.tv/lucky-day-testimonials.html

In the above website, see especially the section on Horse-Racing.

Also see the ruler of the planetary hour range of time for your date, place and time when you will bet the race. If the ruler of the planetary hour happens to be Jupiter or Venus, that's encouraging news for you.

Day planetary hours are intervals of time (i.e. the solar time shown on your watch) from sunrise to sunset and you get these intervals by dividing the total amount of time from sunrise to sunset by 12. Night planetary hours are intervals of time from sunset to sunrise and you get these intervals by dividing the total amount of time from sunset to sunrise by 12. In arriving at the length of intervals of time this way, you can see that a planetary hour is not usually an hour of time, unless the day has 12 hours of light and 12 hours of night on the Spring or Fall Equinox.

Each interval of time is governed by a planet depending on the day of the week. If the time when you play a day race is within an interval governed by Jupiter or Venus, there is somewhat more luck in the tendency to pick a winner. For a week, day planetary hours start at sunrise on Sunday morning and they start appropriately with the Sun being the first governing planetary body of the first planetary hour interval of time. On Monday at sunrise, the Moon is the first governing body of the first planetary hour interval of time. On Tuesday, it is Mars, on Wednesday it is Mercury, on Thursday it is Jupiter, on Friday it is Venus and on Saturday it is Saturn.

After the Sun on Sunday, the second interval is governed by Venus, the third interval is governed by Mercury, the fourth interval is governed by the Moon, the fifth interval is governed by Saturn, the sixth interval is governed by Jupiter, the seventh interval is governed by Mars, and the eighth interval is governed by the Sun again followed by the order of the next four planets as described above until all 12 planetary hours are covered and sunset begins. The same sequence of planets governing planetary hours applies to the night planetary hours of Sunday, except that the intervals of time start at sunset on Sunday and end at sunrise on Monday.

At sunrise on Monday, the Moon becomes the first governing planetary body of the first interval of time, the second interval is governed by Saturn, the third interval is governed by Jupiter, the fourth interval is governed by Mars, the fifth interval is governed by the Sun, the sixth interval is governed by Venus, the seventh interval is governed by Mercury and the eighth interval is governed by the Moon again followed by the order of the next four planets as described above until all 12 planetary hours are covered and sunset begins. The same sequence of planets governing planetary hours applies to the night planetary hours of Monday, except that the intervals of time start at sunset on Monday and end at sunrise on Tuesday. Then Mars becomes the first governing planetary body of the first interval of time, and so on.

Fortunately, there is a website you can use to quickly see the ruler of the planetary hour interval for your date, your time and your location when you will bet the race. Here is the website:

http://www.astrology.com.tr/planetary-hours.asp

In the planetary hours box, just enter the date, military time you will bet the race, country and city where you are located when you will bet the race and click on the Calculate Planetary Hours button. The ruler will be shown above your data that you just entered. You might want to change the time when you will bet the race to have Jupiter or Venus become the ruler of that time.

One last point on luck. It goes beyond saying but I will say it anyway. If you are experiencing negativity or desperation in your life, this will act against your picking a winner. You must have a positive attitude on life and be optimistic to pick winners.

Chapter 8

IS IT A GOOD RACE ON WHICH TO WAGER?

If the Sun, Moon, Jupiter, Venus, or Uranus in the chart of the race is on an angle in that chart, it is especially good to wager on the race. If Saturn, Mars, Pluto or Neptune in the chart of the race is on an angle in that chart, it not an especially good day to wager on the race. If Mercury is on an angle, or if no planetary bodies are on any of the angles, there are no favorable or unfavorable influences on the race.

It wouldn't hurt to run a sorted astrological speculum of the race using the date, place and post time of the race. If you sort the speculum, you will see a list of planetary bodies in aspect to each other at the four angles of the chart: the Ascendant, Midheaven, Descendant, and IC (Imum Coeli angle opposite the Midheaven) for the date, place and post time of the race. As you go down the list, note the planetary bodies within eight minutes of each other (12 minutes for the Sun and/or Moon with themselves or other planetary bodies). If Jupiter and/or Venus are within eight minutes of other planets, or themselves (or within 12 minutes of the Sun and/or Moon) as you go down the list, it is a good race to wager on. Janus astrology software is used to create a sorted speculum.

Here is how you create and display the sorted speculum of the race. Bring up Janus and create the chart for the race using the date, place and post time of the race. Then go to the Calculate dropdown and select Diurnal Events (Parans) to get the speculum of the chart. Go to the Settings dropdown, select Options, click on Right Ascension and then click OK. The sorted speculum for the chart displays.

Below is the Janus sorted speculum of the race.

Diurnal Events

6th Race Santa Anita Park

6th Race Santa Anita Park
Natal Chart
6 Nov 2009
2:25:00 PM
PST +08:00:00
Santa Anita Race Track CA
USA
118w03'00
34n08'00
Geocentric

Fagan-Bradley
Campanus
True Node

Events sorted by Right Ascension, Natal LST LST 17:37:52, Natal RAMC RAMC 264 28' 03"

Planet/Star	Event	Right Ascen	Sidereal Time	Local Time	Earth Long of Rt Asc
Saturn	Ic	1 37'	0:06:27	20:52:32	20 w54'
Moon's North Node	Set	9 59'	0:39:57	21:25:56	12 w32'
Venus	Ic	27 08'	1:48:32	22:34:20	4 e37'
Mars	Rise	28 46'	1:55:04	22:40:51	6 e15'
Jupiter	Set	39 28'	2:37:52	23:23:32	16 e57'
Sun	Ic	42 11'	2:48:43	23:34:22	19 e40'
Mercury	Ic	43 10'	2:52:39	23:38:17	20 e39'
Neptune	Set	46 25'	3:05:39	23:51:14	23 e54'
Aldebaran	Mc	69 50'	4:39:21	1:28:37	47 e19'
Uranus	Set	81 28'	5:25:51	2:14:59	58 e57'
Saturn	Rise	90 34'	6:02:15	2:51:17	68 e03'
Pluto	Ic	91 32'	6:06:07	2:55:09	69 e01'
Moon	Mc	99 35'	6:38:20	3:27:17	77 e04'
Moon's North Node	Ic	115 23'	7:41:33	4:30:19	92 e52'
Venus	Rise	123 46'	8:15:02	5:03:43	101 e15'
Mars	Mc	132 37'	8:50:27	5:39:02	110 e06'
Jupiter	Ic	140 56'	9:23:45	6:12:14	118 e25'
Sun	Rise	143 34'	9:34:15	6:22:43	121 e03'
Mercury	Rise	144 45'	9:38:58	6:27:25	122 e14'
Neptune	Ic	146 09'	9:44:38	6:33:03	123 e38'
Aldebaran	Set	171 31'	11:26:04	8:14:13	149 e00'
Uranus	Ic	173 51'	11:35:23	8:23:31	151 e20'
Saturn	Mc	181 37'	12:06:27	8:54:30	159 e06'
Pluto	Rise	194 24'	12:57:37	9:45:31	171 e53'
Venus	Mc	207 08'	13:48:32	10:36:18	175 w23'
Moon	Set	207 32'	13:50:08	10:37:54	174 w59'
Moon's North Node	Rise	220 47'	14:43:08	11:30:45	161 w44'
Sun	Mc	222 11'	14:48:43	11:36:19	160 w20'
Mercury	Mc	223 10'	14:52:39	11:40:15	159 w21'
Mars	Set	236 27'	15:45:50	12:33:16	146 w03'
Jupiter	Rise	242 24'	16:09:38	12:57:01	140 w06'
Neptune	Rise	245 54'	16:23:37	13:10:57	136 w37'
Aldebaran	Ic	249 50'	16:39:21	13:26:39	132 w41'
Uranus	Rise	266 14'	17:44:56	14:32:03	116 w17'
Pluto	Mc	271 32'	18:06:07	14:53:11	110 w59'
Saturn	Set	272 40'	18:10:40	14:57:43	109 w51'
Moon	Ic	279 35'	18:38:20	15:25:19	102 w56'
Venus	Set	290 30'	19:22:01	16:08:52	92 w01'
Moon's North Node	Mc	295 23'	19:41:33	16:28:21	87 w08'
Sun	Set	300 48'	20:03:12	16:49:56	81 w43'
Mercury	Set	301 35'	20:06:21	16:53:04	80 w56'
Mars	Ic	312 37'	20:50:27	17:37:04	69 w54'
Jupiter	Mc	320 56'	21:23:45	18:10:16	61 w35'
Neptune	Mc	326 09'	21:44:38	18:31:05	56 w22'
Aldebaran	Rise	328 10'	21:52:39	18:39:06	54 w21'
Pluto	Set	348 39'	23:14:38	20:00:51	33 w52'
Moon	Rise	351 38'	23:26:32	20:12:44	30 w53'
Uranus	Mc	353 51'	23:35:23	20:21:33	28 w40'

Looking down the Sidereal Time column, planets are in aspect if they are within 8 minutes of each other. They are in aspect to the Sun and the Moon if they are within 12 minutes of the Sun and/or the Moon. The Sun and the Moon are in aspect to each other if they are within 12 minutes of each other.

We can see the following aspects:

- Venus at 01:48:32 on the IC angle is square Mars at 01:55:04 on the Ascendant rise angle.
- Jupiter at 2:37:52 on the Descendant angle is square the Sun at 2:48:43 on the IC angle and the Sun is conjunct Mercury at 2:52:39 on the IC angle.
- Saturn at 6:02:15 on the Ascendant rise angle is square Pluto at 6:06:07 on the IC angle.
- Jupiter at 9:23:45 on the IC angle is square the Sun at 9:34:15 on the Ascendant rise angle, and the Sun is conjunct Mercury at 9:38:58 on the Ascendant angle, and Mercury is square Neptune at 9:44:38 on the IC angle.
- Venus at 13:48:32 on the MC angle is square the Moon at 13:50:08 on the Descendant angle.
- The Sun at 14:48:43 on the MC angle is conjunct Mercury at 14:52:39 on the MC angle.
- Pluto at 18:06:07 on the MC is square Saturn at 18:10:40 on the Descendant angle.
- The Sun at 20:03:12 on the Descendant angle is conjunct Mercury at 20:06:21 on the Descendant angle.

As you can see, there are aspects involving benefic planets for the most part rather than aspects involving malefic planets so I would say the race is a good one on which to wager.

Chapter 9

OPEN A WAGERING ACCOUNT

To bet: DRF bets 1-877-408-1999 (easy to fund by sending them a check; if you wire money into the account this will cost you more; if you use a credit card you will get charged even more and your credit card bank will also charge you for the cash advance).
To bet: Xpressbet 1-866-889-7737 (same as above and also less of a chance of getting locked out on making a bet).
To bet: www.hpibet.com.

Chapter 10

WATCH THE RACE

To watch the race on TV, use TVG -Horse Race Wagering and TV Programming. To open an account call 1-888-752-9884. Make sure you can get TVG from your cable provider. For example, for the 10021 zipcode: TVG is available on Direct TV channel 602, Dish Network channel 399, RCN channel 387, Verizon channel 315, etc. You will view a race every 5 minutes or so of the races shown in the Daily Racing Form at many tracks. Even Irish races in the morning!

Free NYRA TV for NYS races (Belmont, Saratoga and Aqueduct) on Time Warner channel 1994, on Verizon it is the MSG channel, Direct TV - channel 635. On NYRA TV, don't miss Andy Serling's commentary "Talkin' Horses" the morning of the day's upcoming races. NYRA TV also provides vivid displays of post parades so you can see the horses before the race more clearly.

Probably for a big racing day like the Belmont Stakes, NBC SN (Sports Network) will carry all the races on NBC TV for free at Belmont that day. Could also be on CBS TV or ABC TV.

Using the remote, you can switch between the above three to get more information about the race. You will also want to see the post parade of horses from the paddock to the starting gate to see how they look. Before a race, switch the channels until you clearly see the post parade.

You can go to a Simulcast center to see races as they actually occur at screens where you are seated, but get there early to secure your viewing seat. A good one is at Aqueduct racetrack in Queens, NY. When races are simulcast from Saratoga, Aqueduct becomes known as Aquetoga. You can see a list of Simulcast centers by doing an online search. Other good ones are the Turf Club at Center City in Philadelphia and the Meadowlands in NJ. Casinos often have Simulcast centers. You may not be able to see the Arlington Million or the Arlington Million Preview a month earlier unless you go to a Simulcast center.

Of course you can go to the racetrack that has the race and personally partake of the Sport of Kings (and Queens of course!). You'll be able to actually view each horse during the post parade before the race. Horses that are wet i.e. sweating are not likely to win. You want that cool, alert, bold and determined look! You can use your laptop on the day of the race to implement the WIN strategy and to download information about the horses in the card. In the crowd during a race, you might also hear in a deep Jamaican accent "Yo Seven, Get Past That Blood Clot Mon" and perhaps a high-pitched "Let's Go Seven" over and over again. Horse races are very emotional events! There is nothing like hearing the roar of the crowd as the horses come around the eighth pole heading down the home stretch to the finish line.

Afterword

If you haven't yet noticed upon reading this book, the name Midday of the filly from Great Britain I picked as the winner of the 6th race on Breeders' Cup day, November 9, 2006 at Santa Anita Park, is another word for Midheaven which is the term that describes the highest point overhead in the sky traversed by the Sun at noon. In Sidereal Astrology, the Midheaven is the most important point in the chart. For basic and easy-to-understand information on the meaning and use of the Midheaven, see *Western Sidereal Astrology for Beginners* by John Savarese available at Amazon from www.myprimaries.com. This book also explains how the sidereal time values in a sorted speculum are derived and it is a great source for learning the basics of Western Sidereal Astrology.

Resources

To learn more about John Mazurek, go to http://www.countgramalkin.com/gramalkins_resume.html and scroll down to sections on John Mazurek. You will also learn about Count Gramalkin and Cyril Fagan. Also check out:

> http://www.gramalkin.com/printable_versions/soulnars_sidereal_astrology.pdf

For the creation of Solar Fire Fagan-Allen sidereal astrology system and Campanus house astrological charts, use Solar Fire v9.0.22 and above available from www.alabe.com.

SOLAR FIRE SETTINGS:

House System: Campanus
Zodiac: Fagan-Allen
Coordinate System: Geocentric
Angle Progressions: Naibod in RA
Lunar Node: True Mode
Default Houses (Sidereal): Campanus
Default Zodiac: Sidereal (Vedic)
Ayanamsa for Sidereal Charts: Fagan-Allen

Composite Chart Houses: Anchor on 10th House
Display Options: Proportional Houses OFF

For the creation of Janus Fagan-Bradley sidereal astrology and Campanus house charts, and sorted astrological speculums, use Janus astrology software v4.3 and above available from www.astrology-house.com.

JANUS 4.3 SETTINGS:

House System: Campanus
Coordinates: Geocentric
Zodiac: Fagan-Bradley
Moon's Node: True

Notes

Notes

Notes

42443606R00042

Made in the USA
Middletown, DE
11 April 2017